D0913986

Studies in Liturgical Musicology
Edited by Dr. Robin A. Leaver

1. Frans Brouwer and Robin A. Leaver (eds.). *Ars et Musica in Liturgia: Essays Presented to Casper Honders on His Seventieth Birthday*. 1994.
2. Steven Plank. *"The Way to Heavens Doore": An Introduction to Liturgical Process and Musical Style*. 1994.
3. Thomas Allen Seel. *A Theology of Music for Worship Derived from the Book of Revelation*. 1995.
4. David W. Music. *Hymnology: A Collection of Source Readings*. 1996.
5. Ulrich Meyer. *Biblical Quotation and Allusion in the Cantata Libretti of Johann Sebastian Bach*. 1997.
6. D. Dewitt Wasson. *Hymntune Index and Related Hymn Materials*. 1998.
7. David W. Music. *Instruments in Church: A Collection of Source Documents*. 1998.
8. William T. Flynn. *Medieval Music as Medieval Exegesis*. 1999.
9. Margot Ann Greenlimb Woolard (ed.). *Daniel Gottlob Türk on the Role of the Organist in Worship (1787)*. 2000.
10. Tina M. Schneider. *Hymnal Collections of North America*. 2003.

Hymnal Collections of North America

Tina M. Schneider

Studies in Liturgical Musicology, No. 10

The Scarecrow Press, Inc.
Lanham, Maryland, and Oxford
2003

SCARECROW PRESS, INC.

Published in the United States of America
by Scarecrow Press, Inc.
A Member of the Rowman & Littlefield Publishing Group
4501 Forbes Boulevard, Suite 200, Lanham, MD 20706
www.scarecrowpress.com

PO Box 317
Oxford
OX2 9RU, UK

Copyright © 2003 by Tina M. Schneider

All rights reserved. No part of this publication may be reproduced, stored in a retrieval system, or transmitted in any form or by any means, electronic, mechanical, photocopying, recording, or otherwise, without the prior permission of the publisher.

British Library Cataloguing in Publication Information Available

Library of Congress Cataloging-in-Publication Data

Schneider, Tina M., 1973-
Hymnal collections of North America / Tina M. Schneider.
p. cm. — (Studies in liturgical musicology ; no. 10)
Includes bibliographical references and index.
ISBN 0-8108-4706-X (hardcover : alk. paper)
1. Libraries—United States—Special collections—Hymns. 2. Libraries—Canada—Special collections—Hymns. 3. Hymns—United States—Library resources. 4. Hymns—Canada—Library resources. I. Title. II. Series.
ML136.A1S35 2003
026'.26423--dc21

2002154948

The paper used in this publication meets the minimum requirements of American National Standard for Information Sciences—Permanence of Paper for Printed Library Materials, ANSI/NISO Z39.48-1992.
Manufactured in the United States of America.

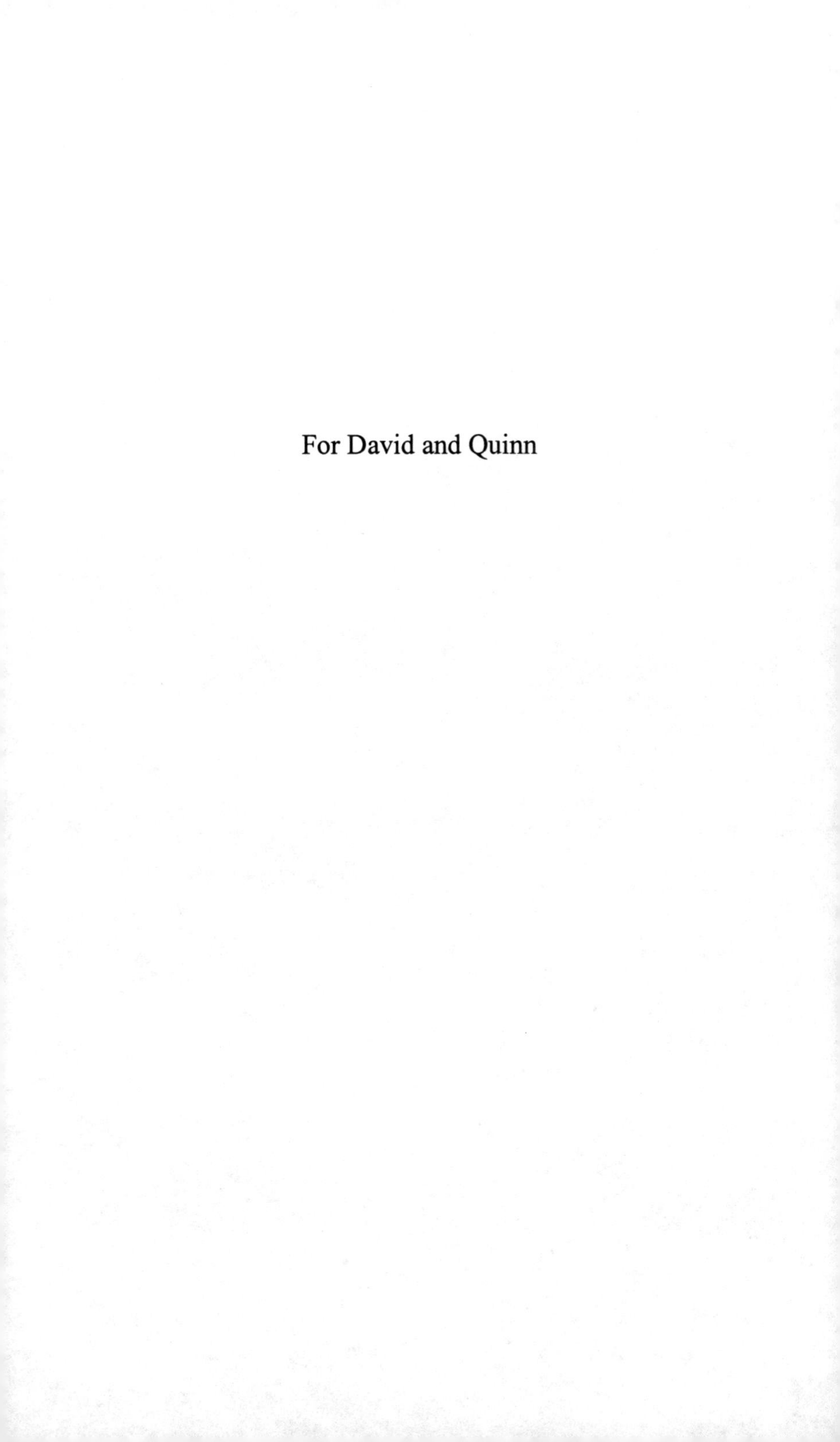

For David and Quinn

Contents

Editor's Foreword

Hymnals are more elusive than many recognize. Since different hymnals can be found stacked on pianos, or filling shelves in bookcases, it is assumed that they are easily accessible. That may be the case with regard to the hymnals in current use, or even to the editions that immediately preceded them. But older hymnals can be very difficult to find also, including some nineteenth-century hymnals that were issued in many editions with extensive print runs. This is because these anthologies of hymns share characteristics of printed "ephemera"—materials, such as broadsides and pamphlets whose "shelf-life" is temporary.

Hymnals generally last for a generation or so, and although some last much longer even they are eventually replaced. Old hymnals frequently get trashed not simply because they are out-of-date, but because they have become worn-out with use and have pages torn and missing. Thus many hymnals that were once available in quantity have become relatively rare, some of them extremely so.

The other problem is that there are so many hymnals that even for libraries it is only possible to assemble a representative rather than an exhaustive collection. Thus even if one has access to an extensive hymnal collection— such as the Benson Collection in Speer Library, Princeton Theological Seminary, or the Warrington Collection in Pitt Theology Library of Candler School of Theology, Emory University— it will not provide access to all the hymnals of any given type. Therefore it is necessary to locate other collections where the desired materials may be found. The purpose of this book is to list the major library collections of hymnals in North America, as well as those collections in private hands where the owner is willing to allow some kind of access to researchers.

Hymnals are more than anthologies of hymns, they are also markers of the theology, spirituality and worship-ideals of any given period. Rarely are hymns transmitted in the textual forms that their authors originally gave them. Editors have for generations altered and re-altered the texts of hymns, adding stanzas and subtracting others, altering their meters, and even making new hymns from fragments of a variety of other hymns. Thus the first-line index may indicate that a hymnal includes a certain hymn, but until the actual hymnal has been examined it can't be known whether the exact form of the hymn is what the searcher expects.

Similarly, hymn tunes frequently exist in many variant forms. Therefore, there is the need to consult earlier hymnals to discover in which form(s) the text and/or tune of a hymn have been circulated. In order to consult these earlier hymnals one needs to know where they can be found—and hence this book. Tina Schneider has compiled this essential tool that will be welcomed by all who need to trace with accuracy the published course of a hymn text or hymn tune.

Robin A. Leaver, Series Editor
Westminster Choir College of Rider University
and The Julliard School, New York

Acknowledgements

A directory such as *Hymnal Collections* could not exist without the generous participation of the collection owners and caretakers. Some owners displayed extraordinary patience as I contacted them twice or even three times with questions about their collections, and I thank them. Samuel S. Hill's *Handbook of Denominations in the United States* has been invaluable to me in tracing the tangled threads of various denominations; the libraries of the United Methodist Church and the Evangelical Lutheran Church in America have also provided detailed information about their various mergers. Any errors in the indexing of these various denominations are, of course, my own.

I must mention the unwavering support of Carl Daw, who suggested this revision to me. I am grateful for his words of encouragement, especially when my progress was painfully slow. Martha Smalley at Yale Divinity School generously allowed me to take material about some collections from her website. Lori Schleeter filled my many interlibrary loan requests with great patience, and Trisha Davis gave unselfishly of her time and expertise. My husband David has been wonderful in listening to me talk endlessly about *Hymnal Collections,* and our young son Quinn has been wonderful in showing me this publication doesn't matter to him at all.

Reader's Note

Hymnals can be tough to find. Many are uncataloged, many are located in private collections, and many are kept in unusual places. Previous editors Louis Voigt and Ellen Jane Lorenz Porter recognized the importance of a directory for hymnal collections; they saw the need for a reference work that provides the much-needed guidance in tracking down items that have not made (and may never make) their way into a catalog. The last version of *Hymnal Collections* came out in 1988. This edition owes much to the information supplied there; without it, many valuable resources might have been overlooked.

While this directory does not necessarily identify specific items, it does point the researcher in what is hoped to be the right direction. Indexes that include denominations, languages, and types of hymnals are all meant to provide some structure to the many collections listed here.

The entries are arranged alphabetically by state/province, city, and then name of the institution or last name of collection owner as needed. Some libraries offer their hymnals through interlibrary loan, but many do not, due to the fragile nature of their holdings. Therefore, I thought it would be of greater interest to the researcher to see what was readily available in the area, and then investigate the opportunities for travel. D. W. Krummel's *Resources of American Music History: A Directory of Source Materials from Colonial Times to World War II* is also an invaluable tool for finding collections of music and related materials.

The descriptions of the collections were provided by the parties responsible for them; I did not write them, although I edited for clarity. I took some liberties in making the contact information as generic as possible, so that the information provided here would last a little longer. If there was no generic point of contact, I included the appropriate job title with the contact person's name when possible.

I have also included institutional entries from the 1988 version for which I did not receive updated information. They are marked with a [1988] in their headings, and there is no guarantee that the information provided is still correct. My thought was that perhaps some collections might still be where they were in 1988, and if not, the institutions might be able to guide the researcher to their current owners. Only one 1988 institution specifically asked not to be included in this edition, and I have honored its request. I have added websites and e-mail addresses for the 1988 entries when possible. Also, the Copy, Lend, Size, and Date Range fields are new, so this information might not be available for the 1988 listings.

Many collection owners listed denominations that are represented by their collections. I have taken them at their word. For example, if an institution affiliated with the Lutheran Church–Missouri Synod (LCMS) listed "Lutheran" as a denomination represented by their collection, I did not assume that they meant only the LCMS, but that they possibly owned materials from other Lutheran denominations as well. Also, if a description mentioned a denomination that did not seem particularly well represented elsewhere, even if the collection had only a few such items, I added it to the index of denominations. You never know what someone will be looking for.

I should also clarify how I am using the term *denomination*. In most cases it is used to identify commonly recognized denominational names (Baptist, Methodist, Presbyterian, Reformed, etc.) but is also used in reference to other religious entities. It is meant as a "catchall term [that] may simply be the best available label for the wide-ranging treatment of religious bodies in America."[1]

Notes

1. Samuel S. Hill, *Handbook of Denominations in the United States*. New 10th ed. (Nashville, Tenn.: Abingdon Press, 1995), 31.

Entries

Entries are in alphabetical order by U.S. state and Canadian province, then city, and then name of institution or owner as needed.

Alabama

1. Samford University
800 Lakeshore Dr.
Birmingham, Alabama 35209
Contact: Paul A. Richardson, Division of Music
Ph: (205) 726-2496
Fax: (205) 726-2165
E-mail: parichar@samford.edu
Web: www.samford.edu

Institutional, Private
Size: 2,000
Date Range: 19th–early 20th
Lend: No
Copy: Yes

Details: E. S. Lorenz and Tullar-Meredith Hymnal Collections: Most materials relate to gospel song of the late nineteenth and early twentieth centuries. The Lorenz Collection was given to Samford University in 1976 by Geoffrey and Steve Lorenz. The materials in the collection are presently housed in the Division of Music, School of Performing Arts, and are not cataloged. It is anticipated that they will be moved to the university library and incorporated into its holdings and catalog.

2. Roger Hicks
13100 Oak Forge Dr.
Mobile, Alabama 36608
Ph: (251) 634-1379
E-mail: rogerhicks@quixnet.net

Individual
Size: 200
Date Range: 17th–20th
Lend: No
Copy: See details below

Details: Items will be copied if able to do so without risking damage to bindings.

Denominations: *Methodist*

Alaska

3. University of Alaska, Fairbanks
Elmer E. Rasmuson Library
310 Tanana Dr.
Fairbanks, Alaska 99705
Contact: Curator of Rare Books and Manuscripts
Ph: (907) 474-6671
E-mail: fftpl@aurora.alaska.edu
Web: www.uaf.edu/library

Institutional, Public
Size: See details below
Date Range: 19th–20th
Lend: See details below
Copy: See details below

Details: In 1988, the size of the collection was estimated to be 350. A current estimate was unavailable for this edition due to construction in the library.

The collection has a few hymnals of various denominations, including Russian Orthodox. Early hymnals produced in Alaskan native languages are of special interest. Many of these are rare books and do not circulate. Upon occasion, copies can be made available.

Denominations: *Catholic, Episcopal, Moravian, Orthodox*

Arizona

4. Gregory Schaefer
6060 North 7th Ave.
Phoenix, Arizona 85013
Ph: (602) 246-9788
Fax: (602) 246-0530
E-mail: schaeferclan1@msn.com

Individual
Size: 700
Date Range: 1610–1900
Lend: See details below
Copy: See details below

Details: *Psalmorum Davidis Paraphrasis Poëtica* (Herborn: C. Corvinus, 1610) by George Buchanan; *Les Pseaumes de David en rime Francoise* (Paris: A. Celleier, 1667), a French Genevan psalter by Clement Marot and Theodore de Beze; *The Whole*

Book of Psalms (London: W. S. for the Company of Stationers, 1633) by Sternhold and Hopkins; and *A New Version of the Psalms* (London: T. Hodgkin for the Company of Stationers, 1699) by Tate and Brady, bound together with *A Supplement to the New Version of Psalms* (London: J. Heptinstall, 1700). Numerous American oblong tunebooks, including important shape-note collections: Little and Smith's *The Easy Instructor* (Albany: Websters & Skinners and Daniel Steele, [1814]); James P. Carrel's *Virginia Harmony* [1836]; Allen Carden's *Missouri Harmony* (Cincinnati: Phillips and Reynolds, 1846); Joseph Funk's *Harmonia Sacra*, 13th ed. (Singer's Glen, Rockingham Co., Va.: Joseph Funk's Sons, 1869); etc. A wide variety of Sunday school music volumes. Important American denominational hymnals represented.

Volumes may be perused at the library site only. Depending on condition, copying of materials is allowed at the library site only.

British Columbia

5. First Metropolitan United Church
Mountford Library
932 Balmoral Rd.
Victoria, British Columbia
V8T 1A8
Canada
Contact: Librarian
Ph: (250) 388-5188, ext. 229
Fax: (250) 388-5186
E-mail: music@firstmetvictoria.com

Institutional, Private
Size: 35
Date Range: 19th–20th
Lend: See details below
Copy: See details below

Details: Local lending only (no interlibrary loan). Copying as condition of item permits.

Denominations: *Methodist, United Church of Canada*

California

6. California-Nevada Conference of the United Methodist Church

Institutional, Private
Size: 60
Date Range: 19th–20th

Archives
1798 Scenic Ave.
Berkeley, California 94709
Contact: Stephen Yale,
Archives and History Librarian
Ph: (650) 952-5177
E-mail: seyale@earthlink.net
Web: www.cnumc.org

Lend: No
Copy: Yes

Details: Various denominations are represented, mainly United Methodist predecessors. The collection includes several hymnals in German.

Denominations: *Methodist, United Methodist*

7. **Graduate Theological Union**
Flora Lamson Hewlett Library
2400 Ridge Rd.
Berkeley, California 94709
Contact: Clay Edward Dixon,
Head of Collection Development
Ph: (510) 649-2509
Fax: (510) 649-2508
E-mail: cedixon@gtu.edu
Web: www.gtu.edu/library
Catalog: grace.gtu.edu

Institutional, Private
Size: 2,100
Date Range: late 19th–20th
Lend: See details below
Copy: No

Details: About 2,100 hymnals cataloged in database, including 1,300 in English, 35 in Greek, 100 in Latin, and 175 in other languages. There are 15 non-Christian items (Buddhist, Hindu, Jewish, and New Thought). One title has German-language Jewish hymns. Some titles are in the rare collection (some pre-1850).

Most materials are available to researchers and visitors on request.

Denominations: *Buddhist, Hindu, Judaic, New Thought*

8. **Claremont Colleges**
Special Collections
Honnold/Mudd Library

Institutional, Private
Size: 3,500
Date Range: early 17th–21st

800 N. Dartmouth
Claremont, California 91711
Contact: Head of Special Collections
Ph: (909) 607-3977
Fax: (909) 621-8681
E-mail: spcoll@libraries.claremont.edu
Web: voxlibris.claremont.edu
Catalog: blais.claremont.edu

Lend: No
Copy: See details below

Details: Robert Guy McCutchan Collection of Hymnology: The collection includes materials from the preparation of *The Methodist Hymnal* (1935). See A. Merril Smoak, "Hymnal Collections in the Greater Los Angeles Area." *The Hymn* 30, no. 2 (April 1979): 102–105.

The collection also includes fraternal, temperance, and patriotic songbooks.

See Special Collections hours on the Claremont College Libraries website, or call to make special arrangements if necessary. Copying is at the discretion of the librarian. Copying is limited if material is fragile or under copyright restrictions.

***Denominations:** Methodist*

9. **Claremont School of Theology** Library
1325 N. College Ave.
Claremont, California 91711
Contact: Reference Librarian
Ph: (909) 626-3521
Fax: (909) 626-7062
E-mail: library@cst.edu
Web: www.cst.edu/Library/RbtMitch.html
Catalog: blais.claremont.edu

Institutional, Private
Size: 8,500
Date Range: 1562–present
Lend: No
Copy: See details below

Details: The Robert H. Mitchell Collection includes 8,500 items; 7,500 are hymnals, books on hymnody, and materials on church music. Unique to this collection are the 1,500 hymnals/prayer books in 210 languages other than English. Among additional holdings are 150 sixteenth- to eighteenth-century books, hymnals, and pamphlets in English, Dutch, French, German and Latin. There are 118 oblong nineteenth-century American tunebooks and 170 oblong nineteenth-century American Sunday school books; a useful reference resource is the collection of 78 books and the companion volumes used by Katharine Diehl for *Hymns and Tunes: An Index* (New York: Scarecrow Press, 1966). Works in French, German, Japanese, Korean, Scandinavian languages, Spanish, Welsh, and a number of Eastern European languages, as well as Chinese, Filipino, Indian, South Pacific (including Southeast Asia and Papua New Guinea) languages, African languages, and Native American languages/dialects.

The library collects materials across the range of chronological periods, denominations, and languages, but focuses efforts on acquiring non-English materials published outside of North America and Europe. A portion of the collection is cataloged and available online. There is a printed shelflist that includes the entire collection. Will copy if condition of item permits.

10. Dona Brandon
1515 Shasta Dr. #1320
Davis, California 95616
Ph: (530) 747-6120

Individual
Size: 275
Date Range: 18th–20th
Lend: No
Copy: See details below

Details: Hymnals and songbooks dating from the 1790s, but mostly from 1850s to the present.

Will copy if book is not too fragile.

11. California State University at Hayward
Media/Music Library
25800 Carlos Bee Blvd.
Hayward, California 94542
Contact: Reference Librarian
Ph: (510) 885-3780
Fax: (510) 885-6049
E-mail: www.library.csuhayward.edu/librarians.htm
Web: www.library.csuhayward.edu

Institutional, Public
Size: 280
Date Range: 19th–20th
Lend: Yes
Copy: Yes

Catalog: See library website

Details: Most materials are available via interlibrary loan.

12. **University of California at Los Angeles**
Dept. of Special Collections
A1713 Young Research Library
Los Angeles, California 90095
Contact: Curator of Rare Books
Ph: (310) 825-4988
Fax: (310) 206-1864
E-mail: spec-coll@library.ucla.edu
Web: www.library.ucla.edu/libraries/special/scweb
Catalog: orion2.library.ucla.edu

Institutional, Public
Size: 700
Date Range: 16th–20th
Lend: No
Copy: See details below

Details: The collection contains 700 cataloged American hymnals, including the George Pullen Jackson Collection of Southern Hymnody (100 volumes) and materials from the Royal B. Stanton Collection. Also contains the Joseph C. Stone Early American Songbook Collection and the Walter Zimmerman Collection of Early American Psalmbooks.

For more information, see: Revitt, Paul, comp., *The George Pullen Jackson Collection of Southern Hymnody: A Bibliography* (Los Angeles: University of California Library, 1964). Available from Gifts & Exchanges, Acquisitions Department, UCLA Library. See also *The Hymn* 30, no. 2 (April 1979): 102.

Rare Books: copying from approved bound volumes is limited to ten pages per volume; copies cannot be made from volumes that have brittle paper, volumes with pages that do not open, volumes which are tightly bound, volumes more than 1 1/2 inches thick, or oversized volumes indicated by a * in the call number.

Open Monday–Saturday 10 a.m.–5 p.m. Send photocopy requests to the Public Service Division of the UCLA Department of Special Collections.

13. **Golden Gate Baptist Theological Seminary**

Institutional, Private
Size: 200

Library
201 Seminary Dr.
Mill Valley, California 94941
Contact: Michelle Spomer, Reference Librarian
Ph: (415) 380-1665
Fax: (415) 380-1652
E-mail: michellespomer@ggbts.edu
Web: www.ggbts.edu

Date Range: 19th–21st
Lend: Yes
Copy: No

Details: Relatively small collection of hymnals. Includes John Hoyt Hickok's *Sacred Harp* (Lewistown, Pa.: Shugert & Cummings, 1832). All regular circulating items are available through interlibrary loan.

Denominations: *Southern Baptist*

14. Oakland Public Library [1988]
Arts, Music, and Recreation
125 14th St.
Oakland, California 94612
Ph: (510) 238-3178
Web: www.oaklandlibrary.org/Seasonal/Sections/amr.htm

Institutional, Public
Size: 130
Date Range: 19th–20th

Details: About 130 cataloged hymnals, from 1880. Most major denominations are represented.

15. California Baptist University
Annie Gabriel Library
8432 Magnolia Ave.
Riverside, California 92504
Contact: Helen Xu, Curator
Ph: (909) 343-4354
Fax: (909) 343-4523
E-mail: hxu@calbaptist.edu
Web: www.calbaptist.edu/library/hymnology.html
Catalog: www.calbaptist.edu/library/nindex2.html

Institutional, Private
Size: 2,500
Date Range: 18th–20th
Lend: Yes
Copy: No

Details: P. Boyd Smith Hymnology Collection: The collection has approximately 2,500 volumes, with many rare and unique items including several early *Sacred Harp* and shape-note hymnals, early editions of works of Isaac Watts, and *A Select Collection of Hymns* (London, 1780), edited by Countess Selina Hastings Huntingdon. It also has multiple editions of the works of Gipsy Smith, Ira Sankey, Philip P. Bliss, George C. Stebbins, Fanny Crosby, and James McGranahan. Dr. Curtis L. Cheek donated his collection of 1,500 volumes of rare hymnals and hymnological texts. Nearly fifty denominations and religious groups are represented. Twenty languages are represented. Titles are continuously added to OCLC's database.

16. San Francisco Theological Seminary [1988]
Library
2 Kensington Rd.
San Anselmo, California 94960
Ph: (415) 258-6635
Web: www.sfts.edu

Institutional, Private
Size: 2,500
Date Range: 18th–20th

Details: About 2,500 cataloged hymnals, including the gospel hymnal collection of Dr. Garth of Pasadena and Dr. Goff of Seattle. Includes negatives pertaining to the "Battle Hymn of the Republic." The earliest volume is dated 1750. There are early Watts hymnals and *Hymns for the Use of the People Called Methodists* (1798). Various missionary publications: Native American, Hawaiian, Eskimo, etc.

Denominations: *Methodist*

17. Point Loma Nazarene University [1988]
Ryan Library
3900 Lomaland Dr.
San Diego, California 92106-2899
Ph: (619) 849-2355
E-mail: reflib@ptloma.edu.
Web: www.ptloma.edu/LibraryServices

Institutional, Private
Size: 150
Date Range: 1880–1940

Details: The collection contains 150 hymnals and songbooks.

Denominations: *Church of the Nazarene*

18. **San Diego Public Library**
820 E St.
San Diego, California 92101
Contact: Bruce Johnson, Supervisor
Ph: (619) 236-5812
Fax: (619) 236-5878
Web: ci.san-diego.ca.us/public-library
Catalog: sdplweb.sannet.gov

Institutional, Public
Size: 162
Date Range: 19th–20th
Lend: Yes
Copy: See details below

Details: The collection covers many denominations, and includes some materials in French, German, and Latin.

Open to visitors and researchers Monday–Thursday 10 a.m.–9 p.m., Friday–Saturday 9:30 a.m.–5:30 p.m., Sunday 1–5 p.m. Will photocopy for a fee and send via interlibrary loan.

19. **Ronald Keeney**
1540 Oriole Ave.
San Leandro, California 94578
Ph: (510) 276-7490
E-mail: keeneyr@worldnet.att.net

Individual
Size: 1,400
Date Range: 17th–20th
Lend: Yes
Copy: Yes

Details: Varied collection. Thirty languages represented. Fifty tunebooks, 100 reference works. Some stable-door hymnals; some shape-note and singing school tunebooks. Mostly American, some United Kingdom and European, covers ninety denominations. A list is available. Includes *The Booke of Psalmes Collected into English Meeter,* by Thomas Sternhold, John Hopkins, et al. (London: printed for the Company of Stationers, 1639), complete but disbound pages; whether bound with a Bible or as a separate book is unknown. Also includes Charles Wesley's *Hymns of Intercession For All Mankind* (Dublin: S. Powell, 1759) and *Hymns For Those Who Seek and Those Who Have Redemption In the Blood of Jesus Christ,* 8th ed., (Bristol: Wm. Pine, 1768). *Psalms, Hymns and Anthems for the Foundling Chapel* (London: printed at the Philanthropic Reform, 1796), with engraved title page. Will exchange duplicates.

Denominations: *Methodist*

20. Henry E. Huntington Library
1423 Oxford Rd.
San Marino, California 91030
Contact: Alan Jutzi, Avery
Chief Curator, Rare Books
Ph: (626) 405-2178
Fax: (626) 449-5720
E-mail: ajutzi@huntington.org
Web: www.huntington.org

Institutional, Private
Size: 550
Date Range: 18th–19th
Lend: No
Copy: Yes

Details: The collection contains 550 cataloged hymnals, including 50 pre-1800 items, mostly tunebooks, and about 500 hymnals and tunebooks 1801–1875.

Open to qualified users only, upon application. Monday–Saturday 8:30 a.m.–5 p.m.

Colorado

21. University of Colorado at Boulder
American Music Research Center
184 UCB
Boulder, Colorado 80309
Contact: Archivist
Ph: (303) 735-1367
Fax: (303) 735-0100
E-mail: amrc@colorado.edu
Web: www-libraries.colorado.edu/amrc

Institutional, Public
Size: 120
Date Range: 1771–1989
Lend: No
Copy: See details below

Details: The Susan Porter Collection is a compilation of material on the dulcimer, plus a collection of early hymnals and tunebooks. If materials are not fragile, they can be used on site, or copied for off-site research for copy costs plus a research fee of $10.

Denominations: *Methodist*

22. Iliff School of Theology
Ira J. Taylor Library
2233 S. University Blvd.
Denver, Colorado 80210

Institutional, Private
Size: 1,000
Date Range: 1800–1940
Lend: See details below

Contact: Marshall Eidson, Curator of Archives
Ph: (303) 765-3179
Fax: (303) 777-0164
E-mail: meidson@iliff.edu
Web: discuss.iliff.edu/taylor
Catalog: library.iliff.edu
Copy: Yes

Details: John R. Van Pelt Collection: Over 1,000 volumes partly cataloged. Some in German and some words-only.

Will photocopy but not mail books. Open to the public and researchers Monday–Friday 1–5 p.m.

Denominations: *Methodist*

23. Municipal Museum [1988]
919 7th St.
Greeley, Colorado 80631
Ph: (970) 350-9220
Fax: (970) 350-9475
Web: www.greeleymuseums.com

Institutional, Public
Size: 150
Date Range: 19th–20th

Details: The museum has 150 hymnals, circa 1833–1975, including many of the Community of Christ and the Church of Jesus Christ of Latter-day Saints, among them *The Saints' Harmony* (1842) and *The Saints' Harp* (1889).

Denominations: *Church of Jesus Christ of Latter-day Saints, Community of Christ*

24. University of Northern Colorado
Music Library
Campus Box 68
Greeley, Colorado 80639-0100
Contact: Music Librarian
Ph: (970) 351-2281
E-mail: musiclib@unco.edu
Web: www.unco.edu/library/music/home.htm
Catalog: source.unco.edu

Institutional, Public
Size: 250
Date Range: 19th–20th
Lend: Yes
Copy: No

Details: Includes hymnals of the Episcopal church, ca. 1820–.

Denominations: *Episcopal*

25. Colorado Christian University [1988]
Library
180 S. Garrison St.
Lakewood, Colorado 80226
Contact: Director
Ph: (303) 963-3250

Institutional, Private
Size: 460

Details: Colorado Christian College description from 1988: The collection contains 460 uncataloged hymnals.

Rockmont College entry [Rockmont merged in 1985 with Western Bible College to become Colorado Christian College, but its entry was still listed separately in 1988]: 200 short-cataloged American hymnals.

Connecticut

26. Connecticut Historical Society
Library
1 Elizabeth St.
Hartford, Connecticut 06105
Contact: Head of Access Services
Ph: (860) 236-5621
Fax: (860) 236-2664
E-mail: libchs@chs.org
Web: www.chs.org

Institutional, Private
Size: 325
Date Range: 18th–20th
Lend: No
Copy: No

Details: See Richard Crawford, "Connecticut Sacred Music Imprints, 1778–1810," *MLA Notes* 27, nos. 3–4 (March–June 1971): 445–452, 671–679.

Denominations: *Congregational*

27. Harriet Beecher Stowe Center
Library
77 Forest St.
Hartford, Connecticut 06105

Institutional, Public
Size: 17
Date Range: 19th–20th
Lend: No

Contact: Librarian
Copy: See details below
Ph: (860) 522-9258
Fax: (860) 522-9259
E-mail: stowelib@hartnet.org
Web: www.harrietbeecherstowecenter.org
Catalog: See website

Details: Seventeen cataloged nineteenth-century American Congregational hymnals, owned by the Lyman Beecher family.

Photocopies will be made depending on the condition of the item.

***Denominations:** Congregational*

28. Trinity College
Watkinson Library
300 Summit St.
Hartford, Connecticut 06106
Contact: Jeffrey H. Kaimowitz, Head Librarian
Ph: (860) 297-2266
Fax: (860) 297-2251
E-mail: jeffrey.kaimowitz@mail.trincoll.edu
Web: www.trincoll.edu/depts/library

Institutional, Private
Size: 1,500
Date Range: 17th–19th
Lend: No
Copy: See details below

Details: English and American hymnals and psalters, including some Native American, about ninety music manuscript volumes. Also manuscript collections of Hartford liturgical composers Nathan Allen (1848–1925) and Henry Wilson (1828–1878). Collection guide: Margaret F. Sax, *Music in the Watkinson Library* (1986).

Will copy but will not mail books; condition may prevent copying of some books.

Open to the public: Monday–Friday 9:30 a.m.–4:30 p.m., Saturday 9:30 a.m.–4:30 p.m. when college is in session (call to confirm). Summer hours are Monday–Thursday 9:30 a.m.–4:15 p.m., Friday 9:30 a.m.–1 p.m.

***Denominations:** Congregational, Episcopal*

29. Wesleyan University [1988]
Olin Library
252 Church St.
Middletown, Connecticut 06459
Contact: Scores & Recordings Librarian
Ph: (860) 685-2660
Fax: (860) 685-2661
Web: www.wesleyan.edu/libr/index.ctt

Institutional, Private
Size: 500

Details: About 500 hymnals, of which 100 are Methodist, including the Carl F. Price Collection.

Denominations: *Methodist*

30. New Haven Colony Historical Society
Whitney Library
114 Whitney Ave.
New Haven, Connecticut 06510
Contact: James W. Campbell, Librarian
Ph: (201) 562-4183

Institutional, Private
Size: 14
Date Range: 18th–19th
Lend: No
Copy: Yes

Details: Fourteen cataloged tunebooks of Daniel Read. Other tunebooks and hymnals used in New Haven.

Open to visitors and researchers (members free, $2 per day for others) Tuesday–Friday 10 a.m.–4:45 p.m.

31. Yale Divinity School
Library
409 Prospect St.
New Haven, Connecticut 06511
Contact: Special Collections
Ph: (203) 432-6374
Fax: (203) 432-3906
E-mail: divinity.library@yale.edu
Web: www.library.yale.edu/div/hymnals.htm
Catalog: orbis.library.yale.edu

Institutional, Private
Size: 2,000
Date Range: 17th–20th
Lend: See details below
Copy: See details below

Details: Lowell Mason Hymnal Collection: Consists of 1,057 hymnals dating from 1660 to 1961. Many of these hymnals were given to the library by Lowell Mason in 1875. Additional hymnals with music were given to the Yale Music Library. Included in the Divinity Library's collection are psalters, metrical versions, Sunday school and children's hymnals, seamen's hymnals, temperance hymnals, hymnals for camp meetings and revivals, denominational hymnals, and hymnals from Yale and the YMCA. Most hymnals in the collection are in English, but also included are hymnals in the following languages: Burmese, Chinese, Czech, Dutch, French, German, Latin, Marathi, Sinhalese, Sioux, Swedish, and Welsh. An additional 1,000 or more hymnals are in the library's regular cataloged collection. A broad range of denominations and traditions are represented. The library will purchase hymnals and collections of hymnals as necessary to provide a representative selection of hymnals for use in connection with the Divinity School curriculum. The catalog records include author/compiler, title, and subject access, and may be browsed by call numbers beginning with HY. There are many additional hymnals in the classified collection at the Divinity Library. A notebook in the Special Collections office contains photocopied title pages for each hymnal in the Lowell Mason collection, arranged chronologically. The Lowell Mason papers, 1813–1980, are available at the Yale Music Library.

The Richard DeLong Collection is now housed at the Divinity School Library as well; it consists of 200 hymnals dating from 1853, with an emphasis on Catholic items. The collection is integrated with regular holdings, but items are identified as part of the DeLong Collection. Personal papers and music manuscripts are housed in the Music Library.

Willing to make a limited number (fifty or fewer) of photocopies for remote patrons. Some hymnals available via interlibrary loan; others are restricted circulation.

Denominations: *Catholic*

32. Yale University
Beinecke Rare Book and Manuscript Library

Institutional, Private
Size: 54
Date Range: 14th–20th

P.O. Box 208240
New Haven, Connecticut 06520
Contact: Public Services Department
Ph: (203) 432-2972
Fax: (203) 432-4047
E-mail: beinecke.library@yale.edu
Web: www.library.yale.edu/beinecke/brblhome.htm
Catalog: orbis.library.yale.edu

Lend: No
Copy: Yes

Details: Five *Bay Psalm Books,* 1640–1758, in addition to other early American items and sixteen other eighteenth-century religious collections. Nineteen nineteenth-century volumes in the Western Americana collection, with Native American hymnals, fourteen Mormon hymnals, and the Charles L. Griffith Collection.

Denominations: *Church of Jesus Christ of Latter-day Saints*

33. Connecticut College
Greer Music Library
Cummings Arts Center
P.O. Box 5234
270 Mohegan Ave.
New London, Connecticut 06320
Contact: Music Librarian
Ph: (860) 439-2710
Web: camel2.conncoll.edu/is/info-resources/greer

Institutional, Private
Size: 40
Date Range: 18th–19th
Lend: No
Copy: No

Details: The library has about forty partly cataloged hymnals representing various denominations.

34. Connecticut College
Special Collections
Shain Library
270 Mohegan Ave.
New London, Connecticut 06320
Contact: Laurie M. Deredita,
Special Collections Librarian
Ph: (860) 439-2654
E-mail: lmder@conncoll.edu
Web: www.conncoll.edu/is/info-resources
Catalog: See website

Institutional, Private
Size: 100
Date Range: 1783–1893
Lend: No
Copy: No

Details: About 100 American tunebooks are housed in Special Collections. Also, several hymnals representing several denominations are in the score collection of the Greer Music Library.

Open to visitors Monday–Friday 1–5 p.m., and by appointment.

35. Stratford Historical Society
967 Academy Hill
P.O. Box 382
Stratford, Connecticut 06615
E-mail: judsonhousestfd@aol.com
Ph: (203) 378-0630
Web: www.stratfordhistoricalsociety.com

Institutional, Private
Size: 36
Date Range: 1801–1883
Lend: No
Copy: See details below

Details: About thirty-six uncataloged volumes from 1801 through 1883 in New England. Emphasis on tunebooks, also hymnals and Sunday school songsters.

Copying depends on condition of item.

36. University of Hartford
Allen Memorial Library
200 Bloomfield Ave.
West Hartford, Connecticut 06117
Contact: Linda Solow Blotner, Head Librarian
Ph: (860) 768-4491
Fax: (860) 768-5295
E-mail: blotner@mail.hartford.edu
Web: libaxp.hartford.edu/llr/UofH_Music.html

Institutional, Private
Size: 55
Lend: See details below
Copy: See details below

Details: Fifty-five cataloged hymnals, including Catholic, Protestant, Jewish, English, German, and Spanish.

Open to visitors and researchers Monday–Thursday 8:30 a.m.–10 p.m., Friday 8:30 a.m.–5 p.m., Saturday 10 a.m.–4 p.m., Sunday noon–10 p.m. Summer and intersession hours vary. Photocopy on premises. Request interlibrary loan from Mortenson Library (li baxp.hartford.edu/llr).

Denominations: *Catholic, Judaic*

Delaware

37. University of Delaware
Hugh M. Morris Library
S. College Ave.
Newark, Delaware 19717-5267
Contact: Special Collections
Ph: (302) 831-2229
Fax: (302) 831-1046
E-mail: askspec@hawkins.lib.udel.edu
Web: www.lib.udel.edu

Institutional, Public
Size: 100
Date Range: 16th–21st
Lend: No
Copy: See details below

Details: The Special Collections include about fifty items with these subject headings: sacred vocal music; hymns, English; or hymns (music format). The library has a collection of about seventy-five song sheets, but only a few are religious.

No lending through interlibrary loan, but will occasionally make photocopies of items depending on condition and copyright status.

District of Columbia

38. Library of Congress
Music Division
101 Independence Ave. SE
Washington, D.C. 20540
Contact: Head,
Reader Services Section
Ph: (202) 707-5507
Fax: (202) 707-0621
E-mail: mdiv@loc.gov
Web: lcweb.loc.gov/rr/perform
Catalog: catalog.loc.gov

Institutional, Public
Size: 16,500
Lend: See details below
Copy: See details below

Details: The Music Division has custody of approximately 16,500 hymnals, tunebooks, and gospel songbooks. Identification and retrieval of these materials is possible through the library's online catalog, the *Dictionary of American Hymnology* (see "Oberlin College, Oberlin, Ohio" entry), the card catalogs of the Music Division, the United States Copyright Office in the Library of Congress, the *National Union Catalog of Pre-1956 Imprints,* and the automated bibliographic utilities that offer access to Library of Congress cataloging records. Hymnals without tunes are found in the library's general collection and the Rare Book and Special Collections Reading Room; hymnals with tunes may also be found in some special collections in the Rare Book Room. In exceptional cases, and only when there are two copies held, the Music Division will loan items for research purposes through interlibrary loan.

Public domain materials may be copied through the Library of Congress Photoduplication Service. The Performing Arts Reading Room is open Monday–Saturday 8:30 a.m.–5 p.m., closed national holidays.

Florida

39. Stetson University [1988] *Institutional, Private*
Jenkins Music Library
Presser Hall, 2nd Floor
421 N. Woodland Blvd., Unit 8418
DeLand, Florida 32720
Contact: Music Librarian
Ph: (386) 822-8958
Web: www.stetson.edu/departments/library/musiclib.html
Size: 105

Details: The library has 105 cataloged hymnals, including Jewish, Episcopal, Mormon, British, Dutch, and German items.

Denominations: *Church of Jesus Christ of Latter-day Saints, Episcopal, Judaic*

40. Hoby Unkelbach *Individual*
6329 Simca Dr.
Jacksonville, Florida 32277
Ph: (904) 743-7579
Fax: (904) 743-7579
E-mail: hoby.unkelbach@worldnet.att.net
Size: 1,300
Date Range: 17th–20th
Lend: Yes
Copy: Yes

Details: First edition *Olney Hymns* (London: W. Oliver, 1779); first edition (and subsequent) of Joseph Funk's *A Compilation of Genuine Church Music* (Winchester, [Va.]: J. W. Hollis, 1832); 4

copies *Easy Instructor,* etc. About 1,000 cataloged hardbacks and about 300 twentieth-century paperbacks.

41. Florida State University *Institutional, Public*
Warren D. Allen Music Library
132 N. Copeland St.
Tallahassee, Florida 32306
Contact: Dan Clark, Music Librarian
Ph: (850) 644-5028
Fax: (850) 644-3982
E-mail: doclark@mailer.fsu.edu
Web: otto.cmr.fsu.edu/~library/home.html
Catalog: www.fsu.edu/~library

Size: 250
Date Range: 18th–20th
Lend: See details below

Details: The collection dates from 1840 to 1900, and consists mostly of tunebooks, some with shape-note notation.

Interlibrary loans are handled through the main library loan office. Music Library loans depend on physical quality of item.

Georgia

42. John Garst *Individual*
123 Fortson Dr.
Athens, Georgia 30606
Ph: (706) 548-3910
Fax: (706) 542-9454
E-mail: esgarst@home.com

Size: 600
Date Range: 18th–20th
Lend: See details below
Copy: See details below

Details: Camp-meeting songsters, oblong shape-note singing-school manuals, paperback gospel songbooks, black gospel material. No catalog.

Lending or copying by individual arrangement with the collector.

Denominations: *Baptist, Holiness, Methodist, Pentecostal*

43. University of Georgia [1988] *Institutional, Public*
University of Georgia Libraries
Athens, Georgia 30602-1641
Ph: (706) 542-3251

Size: 300
Date Range: 19th–20th

Web: www.libs.uga.edu

Details: Includes twenty-five twentieth-century shape-note tunebooks and thirty hymnals. Also, John B. Vaughn Collection (1884–1938), including music manuscripts.

44. Atlanta-Fulton Public Library
One Margaret Mitchell Square
Atlanta, Georgia 30303
Ph: (404) 730-1752
Fax: (404) 730-1757
E-mail: infoline@af.public.lib.ga.us
Web: www.af.public.lib.ga.us
Catalog: afplweb.af.public.lib.ga.us

Institutional, Public
Size: 40
Date Range: 19th–20th
Lend: See details below
Copy: See details below

Details: Slight emphasis on shape-note songsters in the Sacred Harp tradition.

About half of hymnal holdings are available for circulation to Fulton County residents and on interlibrary loan. Others are in the general reference collection or the Georgia History Collection (in-house use only). Self-service photocopiers on premises.

45. Emory University
Pitts Theology Library
505 Kilgo Circle
Atlanta, Georgia 30322
Contact: M. Patrick Graham, Director
Ph: (404) 727-4166
Fax: (404) 727-1219
E-mail: libmpg@emory.edu
Web: www.pitts.emory.edu
Catalog: See website

Institutional, Private
Size: 15,000
Date Range: 16th–21st
Copy: Yes

Details: Warrington-Pratt-Soule Collection: The core of the hymnody collection at the Pitts Theology Library came to Emory University in 1975 from the Hartford Seminary Foundation's library as the Warrington-Pratt-Soule Collection of Hymnody and Psalmody (about 8,700 pieces). Together with what Emory held before this acquisition and what has been added since, the hymnody collection now numbers in excess of 15,000 items. Also in the collection are 2,700 hymnals and volumes on hymnology that make up the Wesleyana Collection. The collection is broadly representative of American and English religious traditions (more than 500 items from Methodist churches, over 350 from Baptist, and nearly 300 from Presbyterian) and hymnal compilers (nearly 200 items by the Wesleys, over 100 by Isaac Watts, over 40 by Lowell Mason), and it includes a rich variety of church music types, from psalm paraphrases (over 600 items) to oblong tunebooks and shape-note hymnals. There are over 7,000 items each from the nineteenth and twentieth centuries and nearly 500 from the eighteenth century. Several sixteenth-century Lutheran hymnals represent the earliest items in the collection. All bibliographic records are searchable electronically through EUCLID, Emory's online public catalog, or OCLC. In the early 1990s, 4,093 embrittled hymnals, printed between 1800 and 1950, were microfilmed as part of the Research Libraries Group's Great Collections program. In 1997–1998, the NEH funded a second preservation microfilming project that encompassed over 600 additional embrittled hymnals, which had been more recently acquired. The hymnody collection is stored with the rest of Special Collections in an area with carefully controlled temperature and humidity and with a dry-agent fire-protection system. As opportunity permits, additional manuscript hymnals and hymnals in non-English languages or from other geographical areas may be collected to complement the core collection.

Denominations: *Baptist, Lutheran, Methodist, Presbyterian*

46. Sacred Harp Museum
162 Oak Grove Rd.
Carrollton, Georgia 30117
Contact: Charles D. Woods, Caretaker
Ph: (770) 787-2263
E-mail: cwoods2002@webtv.net

Institutional, Private
Size: 100
Date Range: 19th–21st
Lend: Yes
Copy: Yes

Details: The collection includes originals or reprints of almost all editions of *The Sacred Harp;* a typed list is available. Other holdings include the most complete original of *The Social Harp* (1855), newspaper clippings on Sacred Harp singing from the

1930s on, manuscript copy of the history of the Chattahoochee convention, and recordings of the Denson Quartet. The museum also has LPs, CDs, cassettes, and videos of Sacred Harp singing.

Materials available only on interlibrary loan.

Denominations: *Primitive Baptist*

47. State University of West Georgia
Ingram Library
Carrollton, Georgia 30118
Contact: Myron Wade House
Ph: (770) 830-2361
Fax: (770) 830-6626
E-mail: mhouse@westga.edu
Web: www.westga.edu/~library

Institutional, Public
Size: 350
Date Range: 19th–20th
Lend: No
Copy: See details below

Details: Annie Belle Weaver Special Collection: Materials relating to *The Sacred Harp* and shape-note singing in general. The collection includes sound cassettes, sound discs, and videotapes.

Open to visitors and researchers Monday–Friday 1–3 p.m. or by appointment. Will photocopy excerpts.

48. Willard Rocker
1180 Washington Ave.
Macon, Georgia 31201
Ph: (478) 744-0824

Individual
Size: 100
Date Range: 1785–1991
Lend: See details below
Copy: See details below

Details: Mostly shape-note tunebooks, 1803–present. Also numeral notation. Some early round-note manuals.

Will copy and lend some materials. Part of this collection is in the Middle Georgia Archives at Washington Memorial Library (Macon, Georgia). Available for scholarly research.

49. Arthur J. Moore Methodist Museum Library & South Georgia Conference

Institutional, Private
Size: 40
Date Range: 1727–present

Repository [1988]
Epworth by the Sea Retreat Center
100 Arthur J. Moore Drive
St. Simons Island, Georgia 31522
Ph: (912) 638-4050
Fax: (912) 634-0642
E-mail: methmuse@darientel.net
Web: www.sgaumc.com/ministries/museum.html

Details: Methodist hymnals and songbooks including Joseph Williams, *A Book of Psalmody* (1729), with manuscript marks.

Denominations: *Methodist*

Hawaii

50. Hawaiian Historical Society
560 Kawaiahao St.
Honolulu, Hawaii 96813
Contact: Barbara E. Dunn, Administrative Director
Ph: (808) 537-6271
E-mail: bedunn@lava.net
Web: www.hawaiianhistory.org

Institutional, Private
Size: 75
Date Range: 1823–1900
Lend: No
Copy: See details below

Details: Seventy-five partly cataloged Hawaiian-language hymnals, 1823–1900, used by Congregational and Catholic missionaries to Hawaii. They are listed in: Bernice Judd, et al., *Hawaiian Language Imprints, 1822–1899: A Bibliography* (Honolulu: Hawaiian Mission Children's Society, 1978).

Open to visitors and researchers Monday–Friday 10 a.m.–4 p.m. Will photocopy depending on the fragility of the item.

Denominations: *Catholic, Congregational*

51. Hawaiian Mission Children's Society
553 S. King St.
Honolulu, Hawaii 96813
Contact: Marilyn L. Reppun, Head Librarian

Institutional, Private
Size: 165
Date Range: 19th–20th
Lend: See details below
Copy: See details below

Ph: (808) 531-0481
Fax: (808) 545-2280
E-mail: mhm@lava.net
Web: www.lava.net/~mhm/lib.htm

Details: About 165 cataloged hymnals in the Hawaiian language, 1823–1898 and later, including some Catholic hymnals. The earliest are words-only. Also about 80 English-language hymnals, and one in Japanese and English. Various articles about Hawaii's hymns.

Open to visitors and researchers Tuesday–Friday 10 a.m.–4 p.m. Will photocopy excerpts. Reprints can possibly be loaned, but not originals. Fragile materials cannot be copied.

Denominations: *Catholic, Congregational*

Illinois

52. Aurora University
Library
347 S. Gladstone
Aurora, Illinois 60506
Contact: Curator, Jenks Collection
Ph: (630) 844-5437
Fax: (630) 844-3848
E-mail: jenks@aurora.edu
Web: www.aurora.edu/library

Institutional, Private
Size: 130
Date Range: 19th–20th
Lend: See details below
Copy: See details below

Details: The Orrin Roe Jenks Memorial Collection of Adventual Materials includes 130 hymnals among 2,000 volumes on the Millerite/Early Adventist Movement (1840–1860) and the later Advent Christian Church (1860–present). These hymnals were for church and camp-meeting use.

Open to visitors and researchers by appointment. Photocopying possible depending on condition of materials. Will consider lending only if second copy.

Denominations: *Advent Christian*

53. Illinois Great Rivers Commission on Archives and History [1988]
1211 N. Park St., Box 515
Bloomington, Illinois 61702-0515
Contact: Archivist
Ph: (309) 828-5092
Fax: (309) 829-4820
Web: www.igrac.org

Institutional, Private
Size: 100
Date Range: 19th–20th

Details: About 100 hymnals of the United Methodist Church and its predecessor denominations. English and German, some words-only, from 1817.

Denominations: *Methodist, United Methodist*

54. Chicago Historical Society
Research Center
1601 N. Clark St.
Chicago, Illinois 60614
Contact: Lesley Martin
Ph: (312) 642-4600
Fax: (312) 266-2076
E-mail: martin@chicagohistory.org
Web: www.chicagohistory.org
Catalog: See website

Institutional, Private
Size: 200
Date Range: 19th–20th
Lend: No
Copy: See details below

Details: The collection contains 200 cataloged songbooks, secular and sacred. Chicago imprints, emphasis on nineteenth-century Sunday school. Some Shaker, some Mormon.

Open to visitors and researchers Tuesday–Saturday 10 a.m.–4:30 p.m. Will photocopy some, unless material is judged too fragile. Will consider exchange, duplicates only.

Denominations: *Church of Jesus Christ of Latter-day Saints, Shaker*

55. Episcopal Diocese of Chicago [1988]
65 E. Huron St.

Institutional, Private
Date Range: 1850–present

Chicago, Illinois 60611
Ph: (312) 751-4200
Fax: (312) 787-4534
Web: www.epischicago.org

Details: Anglican hymnals and chant books.

Denominations: *Anglican*

56. Jesuit-Krauss-McCormick Library
1100 E. 55th St.
Chicago, Illinois 60615
Contact: Reference Librarian
Ph: (773) 256-0703
Fax: (773) 256-0737
Web: www.jkmlibrary.org
Catalog: See website

Institutional, Private
Size: 850
Date Range: 18th–20th
Lend: See details below
Copy: See details below

Details: There is no discrete hymnal collection in the library and no special catalog. There are materials from before the nineteenth century, but many of these items might not be fully identified in the library's card and online catalogs. Lutheran holdings are from both Europe and the United States.

Loan and photocopy service may be available, depending on the condition of the item. No rare books will be copied or made available on loan.

Denominations: *Lutheran, Presbyterian*

57. Meadville Lombard Theological School
Library
5701 S. Woodlawn Ave.
Chicago, Illinois 60637
Contact: Neil W. Gerdes, Library Director
Ph: (773) 256-3000
Fax: (773) 256-3007
E-mail: ngerdes@meadville.edu

Institutional, Private
Size: 300
Lend: See details below
Copy: Yes

Web: www.meadville.edu

Details: About 1,200 partly cataloged volumes related to denominations and publications in the United States, also some English and European items. In a separate collection, about 300 hymnals comprising the collected hymns of Vincent Silliman (1894–1979).

Open to visitors and researchers Monday–Friday 9 a.m.–5 p.m. Will mail, photocopy, and lend via interlibrary loan. Will consider exchange.

Denominations: *Unitarian, Universalist*

58. Moody Bible Institute
Crowell Library
860 N. LaSalle Blvd.
Chicago, Illinois 60610
Contact: Walter Osborn, Reference Librarian
Ph: (312) 329-3572
E-mail: wosborn@moody.edu
Web: library.moody.edu/public

Institutional, Private
Size: 200
Date Range: 1780–1910
Lend: See details below
Copy: See details below

Details: Mostly early gospel songbooks and Sunday (Sabbath) school songbooks. The books are kept in the general collection. A few Ira Sankey papers. There is no particular policy to collect old hymnals or add to this collection. Card catalog only.

Most of the hymnals are in the general collection and are available for checkout and for interlibrary loan. Sheet music, in the Music Library, does not circulate but can sometimes be photocopied. Some rare nineteenth-century Moody-Sankey songbooks are only in the Moodyana Collection and do not circulate.

59. Newberry Library
60 W. Walton St.
Chicago, Illinois 60610
Contact: Library Services Division
Ph: (312) 943-9090
Fax: (312) 255-3513

Institutional, Private
Size: 2,500
Date Range: 17th–20th
Lend: No
Copy: Yes

E-mail: reference@newberry.org
Web: www.newberry.org

Details: 2,500 cataloged hymnals, including the Hubert P. Main Collection of Early American Tunebooks and Gospel Songbooks. Open to researchers.

60. North Park University
Covenant Archives and Historical Library
3225 W. Foster Ave.
Chicago, Illinois 60625
Contact: Director Of Archives and Special Collections
Ph: (773) 244-6223
Fax: (773) 244-4891
Web: campus.northpark.edu/library
Catalog: See website

Institutional, Private
Size: 200
Date Range: 19th–20th
Lend: See details below
Copy: See details below

Details: Hymnals in the general collection are available for loan; hymnals and songbooks held within Archives and Special Collections are noncirculating but are available for on-site use, by appointment. North Park also houses the Covenant Archives and Historical Library, and the Swedish American Archives of Greater Chicago.

If condition of the hymnal allows, Archives and Special Collections will provide some copy service. Contact staff for specifics.

***Denominations**: Evangelical Covenant*

61. Polish Museum of America
Library
984 N. Milwaukee
Chicago, Illinois 60622
Contact: Librarian
Ph: (773) 384-3352
Fax: (773) 384-3799
E-mail: pma@prcua.org
Web: pma.prcua.org

Institutional, Private
Size: 1,600
Date Range: 19th–1960s
Lend: No
Copy: Yes

Details: Hymnals from Poland and Polish American churches, and individual sheet music. Not sorted or cataloged, but includes compositions by many church organists and Polish Americans.

Denominations: *Catholic*

62. University of Chicago
Joseph Regenstein Library/Music
1100 E. 57th St.
Chicago, Illinois 60637
Contact: Deborah Davis, Music and Recordings Bibliographer
Ph: (773) 702-8447
Fax: (773) 702-6623
E-mail: dgdavis@uchicago.edu
Web: www.lib.uchicago.edu/e
Catalog: See website

Institutional, Private
Size: 300
Date Range: 18th–20th
Lend: See details below
Copy: No

Details: About 300 cataloged hymnals, 1772–1940, of various denominations, some words-only.

Will lend hymnals from the general collection via interlibrary loan. Items housed in Special Collections must be used on site.

63. Southern Illinois University at Edwardsville [1988]
Lovejoy Library
Edwardsville, Illinois 62026-1063
Ph: (618) 650-2603
Web: www.library.siue.edu/lib

Institutional, Public
Size: 900
Date Range: 19th–20th

Details: The library has 900 uncataloged early American hymnals dating from 1810, many acquired by purchase of the Essex Institute, Salem, Mass.

64. Church of the Brethren General Board
Brethren Historical Library and Archives
1451 Dundee Ave.
Elgin, Illinois 60120

Institutional, Private
Size: 225
Date Range: 18th–20th
Lend: No
Copy: See details below

Contact: Kenneth M. Shaffer, Jr.
Ph: (847) 742-5100
Fax: (847) 742-6103
E-mail: kshaffer_gb@brethren.org
Web: www.brethren.org/genbd/bhla

Details: Collection includes *Geistreiches Gesang-Buch* (Berleburg: Christoph Konert, 1720) and some publications of the Sauer Press, Ephrata Press, and Brethren Publishing House.

Items in the collection do not circulate. Will make photocopies in accordance with copyright laws and if condition of item permits.

Denominations: *Church of the Brethren, German Baptist Brethren*

65. Elmhurst College
A. C. Buehler Library
190 Prospect Ave.
Elmhurst, Illinois 60126
Contact: Reference Department
Ph: (630) 617-3160
Fax: (630) 617-3332
E-mail: ref@elmhurst.edu
Web: www.elmhurst.edu/library
Catalog: www.elmhurst.edu/library/iopage.html

Institutional, Private
Size: 200
Date Range: 19th–20th
Lend: Yes
Copy: Yes

Details: The Armin Haeussler collection of about 120 hymnals is interspersed in the college collection. The Frederick and Salma Rueggeberg collection of about 40 hymnals is housed in the library's special collections. Will photocopy or lend materials requested via interlibrary loan.

66. Garrett-Evangelical and Seabury-Western Theological Seminaries
The United Library
2121 Sheridan Rd.
Evanston, Illinois 60201
Contact: Newland Smith, Collection Development

Institutional, Private
Size: 1,100
Date Range: 19th–21st
Lend: See details below
Copy: Yes

Ph: (847) 328-9300
E-mail: n-smith1@nwu.edu
Web: www.unitedlibrary.org
Catalog: nucat.library.nwu.edu

Details: Approximately 1,100 volumes. Primarily nineteenth- and twentieth-century American (including some in Native American languages such as Chippewa, Choctaw, and Mohawk) and British hymnals. Also some African American spirituals.

Denominations: *Anglican, Episcopal, Evangelical United Brethren, Methodist Church, Methodist Episcopal, United Methodist*

67. Lincoln Christian College and Seminary
Jessie C. Eury Library
100 Campus View Dr.
Lincoln, Illinois 62656
Contact: Library Director
Ph: (217) 732-3168, ext. 2234
E-mail: library@lccs.edu
Web: www.lccs.edu/library
Catalog: www.lccs.edu/library/hymnals

Institutional, Private
Size: 2,500
Date Range: 19th–20th
Lend: No
Copy: No

Details: Enos E. Dowling Hymnal Collection: A collection of nineteenth-century hymnals that have been digitized and placed online. They are largely Stone-Campbell hymnals containing the texts of over 9,000 hymns from 19 hymnals. It includes the scanned pages of the hymnals, MIDI versions of the tunes, a search engine for finding a particular hymn, and background information about the authors and compilers of the hymns. Print collection of more than 2,000 rare Stone-Campbell Movement hymnals, including nearly 200 from the Restoration Movement.

Denominations: *Christian Church (Disciples of Christ), Christian Churches and Churches of Christ, Churches of Christ*

68. Adrienne Tindall
27250 Meadowoods Ln.
Mettawa, Illinois 60048
Ph: (847) 816-1468

Individual
Size: 80
Date Range: 19th–20th
Lend: No

E-mail: adriennetindall@cs.com **Copy:** Yes

Details: Eighty uncataloged volumes, recent American and English hymnals and supplements, including *Hymn and Tune Book for Church and Home* (Boston: American Unitarian Association, 1869); Park, Phelps & Mason's *Sabbath Hymn Book* (New York: Mason Brothers, 1858); and Lowell Mason's *Carmina Sacra* (Boston: Wilkins & Carter, 1841). Open to visitors and researchers by appointment.

Denominations: *Episcopal, Presbyterian, Unitarian*

69. University of St. Mary on the Lake [1988]
Mundelein Seminary
Feehan Memorial Library
1000 E. Maple Ave.
Mundelein, Illinois 60060
Ph: (847) 566-6401
Web: www.vocations.org

Institutional, Private
Size: 150
Date Range: 19th–20th

Details: Hymnals dating mostly from the late nineteenth century. Some are words-only, others are in Latin. Johann Baptist Singenberger (1884–1924) and his son, John Singenberger, are represented in the collection both in works for organ and in hymnody.

Denominations: *Catholic*

70. Concordia University
Klinck Memorial Library
7400 Augusta St.
River Forest, Illinois 60305
Contact: John Law, Director
Ph: (708) 209-3053
Fax: (708) 209-3175
E-mail: crflawj@curf.edu
Web: www.curf.edu/library
Catalog: See website

Institutional, Private
Size: 600
Date Range: 18th–20th
Lend: See details below
Copy: Yes

Details: Kretzmann Collection and Schalk Collection: 557 cataloged hymnbooks, including gifts of Adelbert E. Kretzmann and the private collection of Carl Schalk. Printed catalog of Schalk, *Hymnals and Chorale Books of the Klinck Memorial Library* (River Forest, Ill.: Concordia Teachers College, 1975).

Open Monday–Friday 9 a.m.–4 p.m. No mail lendings.

Denominations: *Lutheran*

71. Augustana College
Swenson Swedish Immigration Research Center
639 38th St.
Rock Island, Illinois 61201-2296
Contact: Head of Archives and Library
Ph: (309) 794-7496
Fax: (309) 794-7443
E-mail: sag@augustana.edu
Web: www.augustana.edu/administration/swenson

Institutional, Private
Size: 450
Date Range: 18th–20th
Lend: See details below
Copy: Yes

Details: About 450 partly cataloged hymnals, eighteenth–twentieth centuries. Some in English and Swedish. Also nineteenth-century American Protestant hymnals.

Open to visitors and researchers by appointment only. Will photocopy and send hymnals in good condition on interlibrary loan. Will consider exchange of duplicates.

Denominations: *Lutheran*

72. University of Illinois
Music Library
2136 Music Bldg.
1114 W. Nevada St.
Urbana, Illinois 61801
Contact: Richard Griscom, Music Librarian
Ph: (217) 333-1173
Fax: (217) 449-9097
E-mail: griscom@uiuc.edu
Web: www.library.uiuc.edu/mux

Institutional, Public
Size: 350
Date Range: 1771–ca.1900
Lend: No
Copy: See details below

Details: The library has 350 tunebooks and hymnals, some words-only, dating from 1771 to ca. 1900. Most are dated pre-1830.

Will photocopy up to ten pages without formal interlibrary loan request.

73. Wheaton College *Institutional, Private*
Billy Graham Center Archives
Wheaton, Illinois 60187
Contact: Director
Ph: (630) 752-5910
E-mail: bgcarc@wheaton.edu
Web: www.wheaton.edu/bgc/archives/collectn.html
Catalog: See details below
Size: See below
Date Range: 19th–20th
Lend: No

Details: Collection 35: Papers of Frances Jane (Fanny) Crosby Van Alstyne. Dates of coverage: 1862–1915. Thousands of manuscripts of lyrics dictated by Crosby. Most of the manuscripts are numbered and dated. This collection is also on microfilm. There are restrictions on the use of this collection. Volume: two boxes.
Website: www.wheaton.edu/bgc/archives/guides/035.htm.

Collection 38: Ephemera of Daniel Paul Rader. Dates of coverage: 1916–1985. Newsletters, sermon manuscripts, scrap-books, programs, pamphlets, photographs, negatives, brochures, a taped sermon, slides of the Chicago Gospel Tabernacle structure (now occupied by a supermarket), a videotape copy of a 1928 film, thesis materials, etc., documenting Rader's career. The material deals mostly with his radio work and the church he founded, the Chicago Gospel Tabernacle. Additional material includes sermons of other preachers who spoke at the tabernacle, newsletters and magazines published by Rader, newspaper clippings and articles abour Rader, and reports about mission activities around the world supported by the tabernacle. Volume: three boxes (one record carton, two document cartons), audiotapes, microfilm, negatives, oversize materials, photographs, slides, videotape.
Website: www.wheaton.edu/bgc/archives/guides/038.htm.

Collection 130: Ephemera of Homer Alvan Rodeheaver. Dates of coverage: 1916–1937. Several items in this collection relate to Rodeheaver's music publishing company, Homer A. Rodeheaver Company. Also included are newspaper clippings; copies of *Rodeheaver's Musical News;* an audio tape of Rodeheaver singing solos and duets with Virginia Asher, one of which was written by Fanny Crosby; and two letters sent to friends. Volume: one document carton, one audiotape.
Website: www.wheaton.edu/bgc/archives/guides/130.htm.

Collection 138: Ephemera of Hymn Writers and Composers. Dates of coverage: 1878–1975. Microfilmed contents of a scrapbook containing miscellaneous correspondence, photographs, and memorabilia by and about hymn writers and composers. Included are Cliff Barrows, Merrill Dunlop, Lowell Mason, Homer Rodeheaver, Ira Sankey, George Stebbins, and others. Volume: one reel of microfilm, negatives, photographs.
Website: www.wheaton.edu/bgc/archives/guides/138.htm.

Collection 194: Papers of William Howard Doane. Dates of coverage: 1872–1915. Letters to Doane concerning hymn publishing and writing from Ira Sankey, Fanny Crosby, Philip P. Bliss, Philip Phillips, and Dwight L. Moody's daughter-in-law. Also includes a notebook for hymn and sermon references, Doane's will, handwritten lyrics for hymns, and a photograph of Doane, business leader, philanthropist, and hymn writer. Volume: one box, photographs.
Website: www.wheaton.edu/bgc/archives/guides/194.htm.

Collection 322: Papers of Oswald Jeffrey Smith. Dates of coverage: 1890–1986. Correspondence, audiotapes, hymn and poem manuscripts, lantern slides, phonograph records, negatives, photographs, tracts, posters, clippings, scrapbooks, etc., related to Smith's career as an evangelist, pastor, author and editor, hymn writer and poet, colporteur, and promoter of missions involvement. Documents span Smith's education, colporteur work in Kentucky and Canada, and his pastoring at the Dale Presbyterian Church, Toronto Alliance Tabernacle, Gospel Tabernacle of Los Angeles, the Cosmopolitan Tabernacle (Toronto), Toronto Gospel Tabernacle, and the Peoples Church (Toronto). Volume: twelve boxes (4.4 cubic feet), seventy-five reels, eleven cassettes of

audiotape, negatives, phonograph records, photographs, lantern slides.
Website: www.wheaton.edu/bgc/archives/guides/322.htm.

Collection 357: Papers of Percy Bartimus Crawford and Ruth Crawford Porter. Dates of coverage: 1922–1989. Films, videos, audiotapes, correspondence, a book manuscript, sermon notes, and other materials documenting the evangelistic ministry of Percy and Ruth Crawford, particularly their radio and television work. Volume: one document carton, audiotapes, films, phonograph records, photographs, videotapes.
Website: www.wheaton.edu/bgc/archives/guides/357.htm.

74. Wheaton College
Buswell Memorial Library
Wheaton, Illinois 60187
Contact: Reference Archivist
Ph: (630) 752-5705
Fax: (630) 752-5855
E-mail: Special.Collections@wheaton.edu
Web: www.wheaton.edu/learnres/arcsc/1/index.htm

Institutional, Private
Size: 2,300
Date Range: 18th–20th
Lend: No
Copy: See details below

Details: Represents nondenominational evangelical hymnals well, with a strong emphasis on gospel and revival songs. Collection began as archives of Hope Publishing. Includes four eighteenth-century hymnals, beginning with the Wesleys' *Hymns and Sacred Poems,* 5th ed. (London, 1756); about 1,000 nineteenth-century volumes (about 60 volumes are 1800–1850, the rest are 1850–1900); about 1,300 twentieth-century volumes. Very little of the collection is cataloged. There is a computer inventory, as well as a print inventory by title, publisher, and date of publication.

Margaret Clarkson Collection: Papers of Canadian hymn writer and author.

Holdings in the Special Collections do not circulate, but are available for research in the reading room, as long as the materials bear no usage restrictions. Photocopying is permissible if the materials aren't too fragile. Specific information about the hymnal collection or any other holding can be obtained by contacting the reference archivist through the website. If extensive research is planned and a personal visit is needed, please give prior notice.

Denominations: *nondenominational*

Indiana

75. Anderson University
Nicholson Library
1100 E. Fifth St.
Anderson, Indiana 46012
Contact: Richard Snyder, Director
Ph: (765) 641-4280
E-mail: resnyder@anderson.edu
Web: bones.anderson.edu
Catalog: See website

Institutional, Private
Size: 2,000
Date Range: 19th–20th

Details: Some 2,000 volumes total. Approximately 175 foreign-language hymnals, 360 books on hymnody and hymnology, with hymnals from approximately 120 denominations and groups. The collection includes approximately 150 pamphlet-length items. The strength is in nineteenth- and early twentieth-century American publications. This collection was donated to Anderson University by Bill and Gloria Gaither. It was formerly owned by The Hymn Society of America. At this time Anderson University does not have a plan to purchase additional materials to complement or expand this collection. Online records are available.

One collection, the Barney Warren papers (Archives W650 1995), contains manuscript scores, etc. by Warren, a hymn writer associated with the Church of God (Anderson, Indiana) Reformation Movement.

Denominations: *Church of God*

76. Archives of the Mennonite Church
1700 S. Main St.
Goshen, Indiana 46526
Contact: Director
Ph: (219) 535-7477

Institutional, Public
Size: See details below
Date Range: 20th
Lend: No
Copy: Yes

Fax: (219) 535-7756
E-mail: archives@goshen.edu
Web: www.goshen.edu/mcarchives

Details: Books and materials used in the production of:
Coffman, S. F., hymn editor, and J. D. Brunk, musical editor. *Life Songs* (Scottdale, Pa.: Mennonite Publishing House, 1916);
Church Hymnal, Mennonite (1927);
Coffman, S. F., ed. *Songs of Cheer for Children* (Scottdale, Pa.: Mennonite Publishing House, 1929);
Coffman, S. F., ed. *Life Songs, Number Two* (Scottdale, Pa.: Mennonite Publishing House, 1938);
The Mennonite Hymnal (1969);
Assembly Songs: A Hymnal Supplement (Scottdale, Pa.: Mennonite Publishing House; Newton, Kan.: Faith and Life Press, 1983);
Oyer, Mary. *Hymnal Sampler: For Churches in the Anabaptist Tradition* (Findlay, Ohio: Churches of God, General Conference; Elgin, Ill.: Brethren Press; Newton, Kan.: Faith and Life Press; Scottdale, Pa.: Mennonite Pub. House, 1989);
Oyer, Mary, ed. *Festival Songbook*. Used for the Festival of the Holy Spirit, Goshen College, Goshen, Indiana (1972).

Collections:
Mennonite General Conference Music Committee (1898–1971); Mennonite Church General Board (1971–2002); Mennonite Church General Assembly Collection (1971–2002). Thirty-four boxes.

S. F. Coffman (1872–1954) Collection, twelve boxes.
Mary K. Oyer Collection, four boxes.
J. D. Brunk (1872–1926) Collection, three boxes.

Denominations: *Mennonite*

77. Goshen College
Good Library
1700 S. Main St.
Goshen, Indiana 46526
Contact: Sally Jo Milne, Reference Librarian

Institutional, Private
Size: 3,000
Date Range: 1566–present
Lend: No
Copy: See details below

Ph: (219) 535-7426
Fax: (219) 535-7438
E-mail: sallyjm@goshen.edu
Web: www.goshen.edu/library/Hartzler.htm
Catalog: www.goshen.edu/library

Details: Jesse D. Hartzler Music Collection of American Tune Books and Hymnals: Includes materials from 1566 to the present, mostly American nineteenth-century tunebooks and hymnals. The chronological scope of the collection supports the study of the evolution of American religious music from the 1760s to the 1920s. Many works are represented in several editions. The collection covers the rise and development of various religious and social movements. Many of the works include instructional prefaces. The collection is not restricted along denominational or regional U.S. lines. The collection is closed to additions. About 500 reference titles are cataloged and classified. There is a sixty-page preliminary listing of the entire collection plus a supplement of 350 titles added in 1984. When Goshen College purchased the collection in 1968, Jesse Hartzler organized the works into these categories: Sabbath school tunebooks, denominational and standard hymnals, spirituals (words-only or with tunes), class books, shaped and unconventional forms of notes, eighteenth-century imprints, psalmbooks, Negro melodies, gospel songbooks, etc. This remains the only classification of the collection. The collection has been briefly cataloged and can be accessed through the library's online catalog.

Copying allowed only if condition of the book permits. Open Monday–Friday 8 a.m.–5 p.m., Saturday 10 a.m.–1 p.m. during most of the year.

78. DePauw University
Roy O. West Library
400 S. College Ave.
P.O. Box 37
Greencastle, Indiana 46135
Contact: Archives and Special Collections
Ph: (765) 658-4406
Fax: (765) 658-4423

Institutional, Private
Size: 217
Date Range: 19th–20th
Lend: See details below
Copy: Yes

E-mail: archives@depauw.edu
Web: www.depauw.edu/library/archives
Catalog: web2.palni.edu/depauw

Details: Methodism, including various predecessors.

Will loan hymnals located in general (circulating) collection. Hymnals located in special collections do not circulate. Available for research use Monday–Friday 8 a.m.–5 p.m., and Tuesday evenings 6–9 p.m. during the academic year. Summer hours are Monday–Friday 8 a.m.–4 p.m.

Denominations: *Evangelical Association, Evangelical United Brethren, Methodist Church, Methodist Episcopal, United Brethren in Christ, United Methodist*

79. Christian Theological Seminary *Institutional, Private*
1000 W. 42nd St.
Indianapolis, Indiana 46208
Contact: David Bundy, Librarian
Ph: (317) 931-2370
Fax: (317) 923-1961
E-mail: dbundy@cts.edu
Web: www.cts.edu

Size: 150
Date Range: 18th–21st
Lend: No
Copy: Yes

Details: Mostly Disciples of Christ hymnals. Includes hymnals used by circuit riders in the Midwest, ca. 1820–.

Denominations: *Christian Church (Disciples of Christ), Christian Churches and Churches of Christ, Churches of Christ*

80. New Harmony Workingmen's Institute [1988] *Institutional, Public*
Library
407 W. Tavern St.
P.O. Box 368
New Harmony, Indiana 47631-0368
Ph: (812) 682-4806
Web: www.newharmonywmi.lib.in.us

Date Range: 19th

Details: Locally used hymnals and songbooks.

81. Manchester College
Funderburg Library
604 E. College Ave.
North Manchester, Indiana 46962
Contact: Robin Gratz,
Library Director
Ph: (260) 982-5063
Fax: (260) 982-5362
E-mail: rjgratz@manchester.edu
Web: www.manchester.edu/Academic/library

Institutional, Private
Size: 130
Date Range: 18th–20th
Lend: No
Copy: Yes

Details: The Brethren Historical Collection includes eight published Church of the Brethren psalmbooks from late eighteenth and early nineteenth centuries, in German. The collection also includes 120 hymnals, some in German, dating from ca. 1840–1940.

Denominations: *Church of the Brethren*

82. Fulton County Historical Society
37 E. 375 N.
Rochester, Indiana 46975
Contact: Shirley Willard,
Executive Director
Ph: (219) 223-4436
E-mail: wwillard@rtcol.com
Web: www.icss.net/~fchs

Institutional, Private
Size: 300
Date Range: 19th–20th
Lend: No
Copy: Yes

Details: Hymnbooks from local churches, some sheet music, and recordings.

83. Taylor University
Zondervan Library
236 W. Reade Ave.
Upland, Indiana 46989-1001
Contact: Daniel J. Bowell,
Director
Ph: (765) 998-5241
Fax: (765) 998-5569
E-mail: dnbowell@tayloru.edu

Institutional, Private
Size: 200
Date Range: 19th–20th
Lend: See details below
Copy: Yes

Web: www.tayloru.edu/library/upland

Details: The library has 200 hymnals, ca. 1860–1940, including Methodist and interdenominational, in the Ayres Collection.

Denominations: *interdenominational, Methodist*

84. Grace College & Theological Seminary
Morgan Library
200 Seminary Dr.
Winona Lake, Indiana 46590
Contact: William Darr, Director
Ph: (574) 372-5100
Fax: (574) 372-5176
E-mail: wedarr@grace.edu
Web: www.grace.edu

Institutional, Private
Size: 400
Date Range: 19th–20th

Details: The library has many Rodeheaver Music imprints.

Iowa

85. Des Moines County Historical Society
1616 Dill St.
Burlington, Iowa 52601-4008
Contact: Deb Olson
Ph: (319) 753-2449
E-mail: dmcohist@interlinklc.net
Web: www.interl.net/~maryhart

Institutional, Private
Size: 33
Date Range: 19th–20th
Lend: No
Copy: Yes

Details: The collection of thirty-three hymnals includes four in German, four Methodist hymnals, and five Pentecostal hymnals.

Denominations: *Methodist, Pentecostal*

86. Luther College
Preus Library
700 College Dr.
Decorah, Iowa 52101
Contact: Jane Kemp, Special Collections

Institutional, Private
Size: 500
Date Range: 18th–20th
Lend: Yes
Copy: Yes

Ph: (563) 387-1195
Fax: (563) 387-1657
E-mail: kempjane@luther.edu
Web: library.luther.edu
Catalog: books.luther.edu

Details: Many Norwegian American hymnals, ca. 1870–1913.

Denominations: *Lutheran*

87. Vesterheim Norwegian-American Museum
523 W. Water St.
P.O. Box 379
Decorah, Iowa 52101
Ph: (563) 382-9681
Fax: (563) 382-8828
E-mail: vesterheim@vesterheim.org
Web: www.vesterheim.org

Institutional, Private
Size: 350
Date Range: 18th–20th
Lend: No
Copy: No

Details: Numerous hymnals published in Norway. Also Norwegian American imprints.

Denominations: *Lutheran*

88. Wartburg Theological Seminary
Reu Memorial Library
333 Wartburg Pl.
Dubuque, Iowa 52004
Contact: Susan Ebertz, Assistant Director
Ph: (563) 589-0267
Fax: (563) 589-0333
E-mail: SEbertz@wartburgseminary.edu
Web: www.wartburgseminary.edu/campus/library.htm

Institutional, Private
Size: 500
Date Range: 1750–present
Lend: See details below
Copy: See details below

Details: Strong in German and English hymnologies and liturgies from 1750.

Open to visitors and researchers during regular library hours. Will photocopy or lend most material on interlibrary loan (preferably OCLC).

Denominations: *Lutheran*

89. Graceland University
Institutional, Private
Frederick Madison Smith Library
1 University Place
Lamoni, Iowa 50140
Contact: Francis Acland
Ph: (641) 784-5303
Fax: (641) 784-5497
E-mail: acland@graceland.edu
Web: www2.graceland.edu
Size: 120
Date Range: 19th–20th
Lend: No
Copy: Yes

Details: Most of the hymnals are connected with the history of the Reorganized Church of Jesus Christ of Latter-day Saints, now known as the Community of Christ. Many are from the second half of the nineteenth century.

Denominations: *Community of Christ*

90. William Penn University [1988]
Institutional, Private
Wilcox Library
201 Trueblood Ave.
Oskaloosa, Iowa 52577
Ph: (800) 779-7366
Web: www.wmpenn.edu
Size: 300
Date Range: 1910s–1930s

Details: Hymnals represent many denominations. Most are located in the Clarence Pickett and Charles L. Griffith Collections.

91. John F. Moore
Individual
605 E. Washington
Sigourney, Iowa 52591
Ph: (641) 622-2596
Size: 450
Date Range: 19th–20th

Details: One Norwegian, two German, two Swedish hymnals. A general collection that includes gospel hymnals and Bible-camp souvenirs. Several instrumental hymnbooks and books about hymns. Several are pocket-size and words-only. Willing to trade extra hymnals.

Denominations: *Methodist*

Kansas

92. Center for Mennonite Brethren Studies
Tabor College
400 S. Jefferson
Hillsboro, Kansas 67063
Contact: Peggy Goertzen, Director
Ph: (620) 947-3691
Fax: (620) 947-2607
E-mail: peggy@tabor.edu
Web: www.tabor.edu/library/cmbs.shtm

Institutional, Private
Size: 3,500
Date Range: 19th–21st
Lend: No
Copy: Yes

Details: The Heritage Collection includes the Paul W. Wohlgemuth Hymnal Collection and collections of Herbert C. Richert and Jonah Kliewer. The strengths of the collection are the German-language hymnals and songbooks, particularly Mennonite-related, and the gospel songs.

Denominations: *Church of God in Christ (Mennonite), German Baptist Brethren, Mennonite, Mennonite Brethren*

93. University of Kansas
Kenneth Spencer Research Library
1450 Poplar Ln.
Lawrence, Kansas 66045
Contact: Special Collections Librarian
Ph: (785) 864-4334
Fax: (785) 864-5803
E-mail: ksrlref@ku.edu
Web: spencer.lib.ku.edu

Institutional, Public
Size: 1,500
Date Range: 17th–20th
Lend: No
Copy: See details below

Details: The Shull Collection of Hymnals and Music Books is strong in eighteenth- and nineteenth-century German American imprints and contains a very significant concentration of oblong books.

Copying is subject to approval of conservator and curator.

Denominations: *Brethren, Lutheran, Mennonite, Methodist, Methodist Episcopal, Presbyterian, Reformed*

94. Riley County Historical Society and Museum
Taylor and Charlson Archives
Fay N. & Dora Seaton Memorial Library
2309 Claflin Rd.
Manhattan, Kansas 66502
Contact: D. Cheryl Collins, Director/Curator
Ph: (785) 565-6490
Fax: (785) 565-6491

Institutional, Public & Private
Size: 40
Date Range: 19th–20th
Lend: No
Copy: Yes

Details: About forty cataloged hymnals, from 1850. Some words-only. Some Swedish language.

95. Bethel College
Mennonite Library and Archives
300 E. 27th St.
North Newton, Kansas 67117
Contact: Archivist
Ph: (316) 284-5304
Fax: (316) 284-5843
E-mail: mla@bethelks.edu
Web: www.bethelks.edu/services/mla
Catalog: felix.bethelks.edu

Institutional, Private
Size: 800
Date Range: 17th–20th
Lend: No
Copy: See details below

Details: The 800 items in the collection, all used in the United States, were published both domestically (about 250) and in Europe. Strong in German with editions of the *Ausbund* from the seventeenth century to the present.

No lending, but will photocopy depending on the condition of the item. Open to the public Monday–Thursday 10 a.m.–noon, 1–5 p.m.

Denominations: *Mennonite*

96. Pittsburg State University
Leonard H. Axe Library
1605 S. Joplin
Pittsburg, Kansas 66762
Contact: Special Collections Curator
Ph: (620) 235-4883
Fax: (620) 235-4090
E-mail: speccoll@mail.pittstate.edu
Web: library.pittstate.edu

Institutional, Public
Size: 35
Date Range: 18th–20th
Lend: See details below
Copy: Yes

Details: Includes Isaac Watts, *Psalms of David* (Worcester, Mass.: Isaiah Thomas, 1786). One-third of collection is shape-note. Includes temperance hymnals.

Open Monday–Friday 8 a.m.–noon, 1–5 p.m. Will photocopy, mail, and send upon interlibrary loan or other request.

Denominations: *Methodist, Spiritualist*

Kentucky

97. Berea College
Special Collections
Hutchins Library
100 Campus Dr.
Berea, Kentucky 40404
Contact: Steve Gowler, Head of Special Collections
Ph: (859) 985-3272
Fax: (859) 985-3912
E-mail: steve_gowler@berea.edu
Web: www.berea.edu/library/library.html

Institutional, Private
Size: 750
Date Range: 19th–20th
Lend: No
Copy: Yes

Details: Includes 300 early Baptist and Primitive Baptist items dating from 1805. Holdings also include the Gladys James Collection of manuscript hymn tunes collected ca. 1930; and the John F. Smith Collection, which documents singing at the Foundation School (Berea, 1911–ca. 1930), and is comprised of 450 manuscript ballad and hymn texts.

Denominations: *Baptist, Primitive Baptist*

98. Western Kentucky University
Special Collections
Kentucky Library
1 Big Red Way
Bowling Green, Kentucky 42101
Contact: Connie Mills, Coordinator
Ph: (270) 745-6092
Fax: (270) 745-6264
E-mail: connie.mills@wku.edu
Web: www.wku.edu/Library/dlsc
Catalog: topcat200.wku.edu

Institutional, Public
Size: 500
Date Range: 19th–20th
Lend: No
Copy: See details below

Details: The collection includes approximately 200 hymnals with shape-notes, 2 Shaker with letteral notation. Emphasis on Shaker hymnals from the South Union Shaker Community, with eight manuscripts.

Open to visitors Monday–Friday 8:30 a.m.–4:30 p.m., Saturday 9:30 a.m.–4 p.m. Limited photocopying.

Denominations: *Shaker*

99. University of Kentucky [1988]
Margaret I. King Library
Lexington, Kentucky 40506-0456
Ph: (859) 257-9668
Web: www.uky.edu/Libraries

Institutional, Public
Size: 64
Date Range: 1760s–20th

Details: Sixty-four tunebooks and hymnals from Indiana, Kentucky, and Cincinnati. Also nineteenth-century Shaker manuscript songbooks from Pleasant Hill, Kentucky.

Denominations: *Shaker*

100. University of Kentucky
John Jacob Niles Center for
American Music
106 Little Fine Arts Library
Lexington, Kentucky 40506-0224
Contact: Ron Pen, Director
Ph: (859) 257-8183
E-mail: rapen01@uky.edu
Web: www.uky.edu/Libraries/NilesCenter

Institutional, Public
Size: 5,000
Date Range: 18th–20th
Lend: No
Copy: See details below

Details: The Glenn C. and Helen Wilcox Collection is an archive of approximately 5,000 hymnals of which approximately one-fifth are processed and cataloged. The collection contains a number of nineteenth-century tunebooks, shape-note hymnals, a large number of Lowell Mason publications, a wide array of Sunday school/temperance materials, various early colonial materials such as Isaac Watts publications, *Bay Psalm Books* (later editions), Cotton Mather psalm translations, etc. The collection complements musical holdings of the University of Kentucky's Special Collections and Archives located in the M. I. King Library.

The collection is a closed-stacks archive that is available for use within the library. The collection is available during regular library hours seven days a week. Selected materials may be available for copying depending on how fragile the item is.

101. The Southern Baptist Theological Seminary
Music Library
Boyce Centennial Library
2825 Lexington Rd.
Louisville, Kentucky 40280
Contact: David L. Gregory, Music Librarian
Ph: (502) 897-4055
Fax: (502) 897-4600
E-mail: dgregory@sbts.edu
Web: library.sbts.edu/welcome.html

Institutional, Private
Size: 4,000
Date Range: 16th–21st
Lend: See details below
Copy: See details below

Details: Major strengths: American nineteenth- and twentieth-century hymnals; emphasis on Baptist and gospel hymnody. In cludes some words-only. Nationalities and languages represented: African, Arabic, Assamese, Burmese, Cherokee, Chinese, Choctaw, Creek, Danish, Dutch, English, Filipino, Finnish, French, Gaelic, German, Greek, Hawaiian, Hebrew, Irish, Italian, Japanese, Korean, Latin, Latvian, Lithuanian, Mohican, Nigerian, Norwegian, Portuguese, Romanian, Russian, Scottish, Slovak, Spanish, Swedish, Syrian, Taiwanese, Tamil, Telugu, Welsh, Yoruba.

Will send on interlibrary loan; photocopy, but not entire books. Will consider exchange.

Open to visitors and researchers Monday–Thursday 7:45 a.m.–11 p.m., Friday 7:45 a.m.–10 p.m., Saturday 10 a.m.–7 p.m.

Denominations: *Baptist, Southern Baptist*

102. University of Louisville [1988]
School of Music
Anderson Memorial Music Library
2301 S. Third St.
Louisville, Kentucky 40292
Contact: Director of Music Library
Ph: (502) 852-5659
Web: www.louisville.edu/library/music

Institutional, Public
Size: 400
Date Range: 19th–20th

Details: Forty cataloged hymnals, 350 uncataloged hymnals. Includes 50 early American items and Sunday school songbooks (1830s–1840s: Emerson, Mason, etc.) and 150 hymnals from many denominations. About 150 items in the Stamps-Baxter Collection, including gospel songbooks and spirituals.

Louisiana

103. Louisiana State University
Carter Music Resources Library
University Libraries
Baton Rouge, Louisiana 70803
Contact: Lois Kuyper-Rushing, Head
Ph: (225) 578-462

Institutional, Public
Size: 122
Date Range: 19th–20th
Lend: See details below
Copy: See details below

Fax: (225) 578-6825
E-mail: lkuyper@lsu.edu
Web: www.lib.lsu.edu/music

Details: Circulating collection: 103 standard hymnals, 26 of which are pre-1900. Noncirculating collection: 19 hymnals, 10 of which are pre-1860.

All circulating collection hymnals can be borrowed; some of the noncirculating collection can be photocopied.

104. New Orleans Baptist Theological Seminary
Martin Music Library
John T. Christian Library
4110 Seminary Pl.
New Orleans, Louisiana 70126
Contact: Music Librarian
Ph: (504) 816-8018
E-mail: mlib@nobts.edu
Web: www.nobts.edu/library/default.shtm
Catalog: See website

Institutional, Private
Size: 1,000
Date Range: 1619–1998
Lend: See details below
Copy: See details below

Details: Martin-Sellers Hymnal Collection: The hymnal collection of the Martin Music Library contains over 1,000 volumes. Chant, psalters, tunebooks, and hymnals dating back to a 1619 book of chant, a 1651 Sternhold and Hopkins, and Tate and Brady, *A New Version of the Psalms of David* (London: printed for the Company of Stationers, 1706) are representative of the rare collection. The collection continually adds new hymnals as they are published. The collection is dominantly used for research purposes, and is available for study during regular library hours. Particularly strong in Baptist hymnody. The collection development policy is to obtain a copy of every published hymnal.

Rare materials do not circulate. Library staff will make a copy of an item if it is in good condition, but will not copy if the item is in poor condition and copying would cause damage. Items can be used under supervision of music library staff.

Denominations: *Baptist*

105. Tulane University *Institutional, Public*
Maxwell Music Library
Howard-Tilton Memorial Library
New Orleans, Louisiana 70118
Contact: Music Librarian
Ph: (504) 865-8645
Fax: (504) 865-6773
E-mail: musiclib@pulse.tcs.tulane.edu
Web: www.tulane.edu/~musiclib
Catalog: voyager.tcs.tulane.edu

Size: 26
Date Range: 18th–20th
Lend: Yes
Copy: Yes

Details: Among the holdings are eight pre-1801 tunebooks and five Joseph Funk collections.

106. Nancy C. Van Den Akker *Individual*
5113 Lafaye St.
New Orleans, Louisiana 70122
Ph: (504) 286-3845
E-mail: nvandena@bellsouth.net

Size: 400
Date Range: 19th–20th
Lend: See details below
Copy: See details below

Details: Miscellaneous hymnals and songbooks, specializing in Roman Catholic and late-nineteenth- and early-twentieth-century gospel hymnals. Also some books on religious music/liturgy, and some records (LPs, late-twentieth-century, gospel, etc.). Will consider requests for loans or copying.

***Denominations:** Catholic, Episcopal*

Maine

107. Bangor Theological Seminary *Institutional, Private*
Moulton Library
300 Union St.
Bangor, Maine 04401
Contact: Clifton G. Davis, Librarian Emeritus
Ph: (207) 942-6781
Fax: (207) 990-1267
E-mail: cdavis@BTS.edu
Web: www.bts.edu/library
Catalog: bts.library.net

Size: 450
Date Range: 1762–present

Details: A varied collection of hymnals from most mainline Protestant churches, over half from the nineteenth century. About 400 hymnals with music, 1762–present; about another 50 words-only. Card catalog records and some online records.

108. United Society of Shakers
The Shaker Library
707 Shaker Rd.
New Gloucester, Maine 04260
Contact: Leonard Brooks, Director
Ph: (207) 926-4597
E-mail: usshakers@aol.com
Web: www.shaker.lib.me.us

Institutional, Private
Size: 100
Date Range: 17th–20th
Lend: No
Copy: No

Details: Shaker Collection: More than 4,000 published volumes, 650 manuscript volumes (handwritten pages bound in book form), and approximately 8,000 manuscripts (single-sheet handwritten items). The Shaker Collection contains over 100 bound Shaker music manuscripts and some single-sheet manuscripts, mainly from the eighteenth century, which make use of both letteral and standard music notation.

Radical Christian Collection: More than 1,700 published volumes. The Radical Christian Collection contains published hymnals for a few of the represented Christian denominations such as Free Will Baptist, Mormon, Mennonite, and Christian Israelite.

Appointments are required.

Denominations: *Christian Israelite, Church of Jesus Christ of Latter-day Saints, Free Will Baptist, Friends (Quaker), Mennonite, Shaker*

Manitoba

109. Don Thiessen
Box 20123
Steinbach, Manitoba R0A 2T1
Canada
Ph: (204) 326-6230
Fax: (204) 326-6908

Individual
Size: 2,000
Date Range: 1850–2000
Lend: No
Copy: Yes

E-mail: dont@mts.net

Details: About 1,400 in English and 200 in German. The rest are in about 30 languages from all continents. Copy of *Liber Usualis* and replica of Luther's first hymnal. Includes contemporary chorus books. Some oblongs. Visits by appointment. Bibliography available.

110. Centre for Mennonite Brethren Studies
169 Riverton Ave.
Winnipeg, Manitoba R2L 2E5
Canada
Contact: Director
Ph: (204) 669-6575
Fax: (204) 654-1865
E-mail: cmbs@mbconf.ca
Web: www.mbconf.ca/mbstudies

Institutional, Public
Size: 500
Date Range: 16th–20th
Lend: See details below
Copy: See details below

Details: Ben and Esther Horch Music Collection: Rare and fragile items not available for lending. Copying services to be determined.

Denominations: *Mennonite, Mennonite Brethren*

Maryland

111. St. Mary's Seminary and University [1988]
Knott Library
5400 Roland Ave.
Baltimore, Maryland 21210-1994
Ph: (410) 864-3623
Fax: (410) 435-8571

Institutional, Private
Date Range: 17th–20th

Details: Collection includes hymnals and music for liturgical use.

Massachusetts

112. Andover Historical Society
Amos Blanchard House
97 Main St.

Institutional, Public
Size: 40
Date Range: 1721–1900

Andover, Massachusetts 01810
Contact: Research Committee
Ph: (978) 475-2236
Fax: (978) 470-2741
E-mail: info@andhist.org
Web: www.andhist.org

Lend: No

Details: Forty songbooks and hymnals, 1721–1900, including Daniel Bayley, *The Essex Harmony* (1770) and Thomas Walter, *The Grounds and Rules of Musick* (1721).

113. Boston Public Library
Music Department
700 Boylston St.
P.O. Box 286
Boston, Massachusetts 02116
Contact: Diane Ota,
Curator of Music
Ph: (617) 859-2285
Fax: (617) 536-7758
E-mail: Music@bpl.org
Web: www.bpl.org/research/music
Catalog: www.bpl.org/catalog

Institutional, Public
Size: 1,000
Date Range: 16th–20th
Lend: No
Copy: See details below

Details: The collection includes early American tunebooks, some from the nineteenth century. Most holdings may be found in The Boston Public Library's *Dictionary Catalog of the Music Collection* (Boston, 1972; Suppl. 1977). Holdings added since 1980 may be found in the online catalog.

The collection is noncirculating. Photoreproduction depends upon condition and collection.

Hours: Monday–Thursday 9 a.m.–9 p.m., Friday–Saturday 9 a.m.–5 p.m., Sunday 1–5 p.m. (Sunday hours October–May).

114. Boston University [1988]
Music Library
Mugar Memorial Library
771 Commonwealth Avenue
Boston, Massachusetts 02215

Institutional, Private

Contact: Head of Music Library
Ph: (617) 353-3705
Fax: (617) 353-2084
E-mail: musiclib@bu.edu
Web: www.bu.edu/library/music/home.htm

Details: Roman Catholic, Orthodox, and Protestant hymnals. Microfilms and secondary literature. Includes Egon Wellesz's research collection in Byzantine hymnology.

Denominations: *Catholic, Orthodox*

115. Boston University
School of Theology Library
745 Commonwealth Ave.
Boston, Massachusetts 02215
Contact: Research Collections Librarian
Ph: (617) 358-0698
Fax: (617) 353-3061
E-mail: sthrsrch@bu.edu
Web: www.bu.edu/sth/library
Catalog: library.bu.edu

Institutional, Private
Size: 2,700
Date Range: 1566–ca. 1945
Lend: No
Copy: See details below

Details: Nutter-Metcalf Hymnal Collection (NMHC): Primarily nineteenth-century holdings, with a significant number of pre-nineteenth-century books (about 155). All records are full AACR2r-level, early works cataloged by DCRB (Descriptive Cataloging of Rare Books) standards. Authorities such as authors, editors, book-producers and artisans are traced where possible, in participation with NACO (name authority program of the Program for Cooperative Cataloging). Collection has about 2,700 items, ranging in date from 1566 to 1945 and after, and is strong in Methodist works. There is also a good representation of most other Christian denominations. The corpus is especially noteworthy for early Americana and demonstration of the transition of British hymn versions and editions to the "colonies" (subsequently the United States and Canada). Some early hymnals in German, including Moravian works, anthologies of Latin hymns, and occasional books or items in French (early Calvinist), Swedish (Midwestern), early Irish, etc., round out the collection, together with sometimes rare revivalist or camp-meeting materials. The library collects hymnals, books of hymn texts and translations, and liturgical and devotional works relating to hymnology, from the earliest representations and editions to the present. Emphasis is given to additions from original-language sources.

Some correspondence and photographs from C. S. Nutter, including letters to and from a few notable nineteenth-century American hymnists. The archival records for these are available locally (and soon via OCLC) online.

At the end of 1999, the library acquired the hymnal collection of Rev. James Rogers.

Most of the collection is cataloged online. There are no other finding aids, except for the Technical Services Office shelflist cards. The old card catalog is gradually being eliminated, and by now is inaccurate for this collection. The NMHC is for closed-stacks access only. All items may be read in a specially supervised area, under controlled conditions when a staff member is present; copying will be considered at the discretion of the Research Collections Librarian.

Denominations: *Methodist, Moravian*

116. The Congregational Library
14 Beacon St.
Boston, Massachusetts 02108
Contact: Harold F. Worthley, Librarian-Historian
Ph: (617) 523-0470
Fax: (617) 523-0491
E-mail: hworthley@14beacon.org
Web: www.14beacon.org

Institutional, Private
Size: 1,550
Date Range: 18th–20th
Lend: See details below
Copy: See details below

Details: Hymnals of various denominations, some words-only, eighteenth and nineteenth centuries; also includes tunebooks. Fifty-nine Lowell Mason items, 1835–1845. Large collection of American editions of Isaac Watts's publications and several "Dutch door" hymnals.

Lending of materials is confined to items under thirty-five years of age. Photocopying depends on the condition of the item.

Denominations: *Congregational, Congregational Christian, United Church of Christ*

117. Harvard Musical Association
57A Chestnut St.
Boston, Massachusetts 02108
Contact: Natalie Palme
Ph: (617) 523-2897
Fax: (617) 523-2897

Institutional, Private
Size: 70
Date Range: 18th–19th
Lend: No

Details: About seventy partly cataloged hymnals, mostly American and English, including forty eighteenth- and nineteenth-century American tunebooks.

118. Massachusetts Historical Society
1154 Boylston St.
Boston, Massachusetts 02215
Contact: Reference Librarian
Ph: (617) 646-0509
Fax: (617) 859-0074
E-mail: library@masshist.org
Web: www.masshist.org
Catalog: www.masshist.org/catalog.html

Institutional, Private
Date Range: 18th–19th
Lend: No
Copy: See details below

Details: Hymnals are cataloged individually in the online catalog and in the library card catalog. The Shaker Collection is not available for browsing. Please contact the reference librarian with specific requests.

Denominations: *Shaker*

119. Harvard Divinity School [1988]
Andover-Harvard Theological Library
45 Francis Ave.
Cambridge, Massachusetts 02138-1994
Contact: Reference Desk

Institutional, Private
Size: 5,000
Date Range: 18th–20th

Ph: (617) 496-2485
Fax: (617) 496-4111
Web: www.hds.harvard.edu/library

Details: About 5,000 partly cataloged hymnals, from 1713. Many nineteenth-century American (some words-only). Also hymnals in French, German, and Scandinavian languages. Emphasis on Unitarian Universalist hymnals and other liberal denominations.

Denominations: *Unitarian Universalist*

120. Episcopal Divinity School and Weston Jesuit School of Theology
Library
99 Brattle St.
Cambridge, Massachusetts 02138
Contact: Reference Librarian
Ph: (617) 349-3602
Fax: (617) 349-3603
E-mail: reference@edswjst.org
Web: www.edswjst.org

Institutional, Private
Size: 300
Date Range: 19th–20th
Lend: No
Copy: See details below

Details: The Charles L. Hutchins Collection of Hymnology came as part of the merger with the Philadelphia Divinity School. Episcopal hymnals and related choir music, chiefly late-nineteenth- to early-twentieth-century material.

Will photocopy ($1.50 minimum).

Denominations: *Episcopal*

121. Pocumtuck Valley Memorial Association
P.O. Box 53
6 Memorial St.
Deerfield, Massachusetts 01342
Contact: Librarian
Ph: (413) 775-7125
Fax: (413) 775-7223
E-mail: library@historic-deerfield.org

Institutional, Public
Size: 150
Date Range: 18th–19th
Lend: No
Copy: Yes

Web: www.historic-deerfield.org/collections/libraries.html
Catalog: See website

Details: About 150 partly cataloged hymnals published in New England 1780–1890. Unitarian, Universalist, Congregational, etc.; earliest are shape-note. Hymnals by William Bull (1762–1842).

Library open Monday–Friday, 9 a.m.–5 p.m.

Denominations: *Congregational, Unitarian, Universalist*

122. Framingham Historical Society and Museum [1988]
Institutional, Private
Date Range: 19th–20th
P.O. Box 2032
Framingham, Massachusetts 01703-2032
Contact: Curator
Ph: (508) 872-3780
E-mail: curator@framinghamhistory.org
Web: www.framinghamhistory.org

Details: Mostly songbooks, but also includes fifty hymnals from the early nineteenth century.

123. Andover Newton Theological School
Institutional, Private
Size: 600
Date Range: 18th–20th
Lend: See details below
Copy: Yes
Franklin Trask Library
169 Herrick Rd.
Newton Center, Massachusetts 02459
Contact: Diana Yount, Special Collections Librarian
Ph: (617) 964-1100
Fax: (617) 965-9756
E-mail: dyount@ants.edu
Web: www.ants.edu/library
Catalog: See website

Details: The majority of eighteenth- and nineteenth-century hymnals are noncirculating.

Appointments are required for researchers not affiliated with the school.

Denominations: *Baptist*

124. Forbes Library [1988]
20 West St.
Northampton, Massachusetts 01060
Ph: (413) 587-1011
Web: www.forbeslibrary.org

Institutional, Public
Size: 120
Date Range: 18th–20th

Details: About 120 cataloged hymnals, mostly nineteenth-century and from the northeast United States. Includes several late-eighteenth- and early-nineteenth-century tunebooks.

125. Historic Northampton Museum and Educational Center [1988]
46 Bridge St.
Northampton, Massachusetts 01060
Ph: (413) 584-6011
Fax: (413) 584-7956
Web: www.historic-northampton.org

Institutional, Private
Size: 150
Date Range: 19th–20th

Details: About 150 partly cataloged hymnals (12 words-only), mostly from the nineteenth century.

126. Hancock Shaker Village
Amy Bess and Lawrence K. Miller Library
P.O. Box 927
Pittsfield, Massachusetts 01202
Contact: Curator
Ph: (800) 817-1137
Fax: (413) 447-9357
E-mail: curator@hancockshakervillage.org
Web: www.hancockshakervillage.org

Institutional, Private
Size: 25
Date Range: 19th–early 20th
Lend: No

Details: Twenty-five Shaker hymnals published ca. 1884, including Isaac N. Youngs, *A Short Abridgement of the Rules of*

Music (New Lebanon, N.Y., 1846). Six manuscript volumes in Shaker letteral notation from Hancock, Mass., and New Lebanon, N.Y.

Denominations: *Shaker*

127. Pilgrim Society [1988] *Institutional, Private*
Pilgrim Hall Museum **Date Range:** 19th–20th
75 Court St.
Plymouth, Massachusetts 02360
Ph: (508) 746-1620
Fax: (508) 747-4228
Web: www.pilgrimhall.org/plgrmhll.htm

Details: Uncataloged American imprints, 1819–1912. Includes Episcopal and Congregational psalmbooks, singing school and Sunday school material. Items by Lowell Mason, and a reprint of the *Bay Psalm Book* (1640).

Denominations: *Congregational, Episcopal*

128. Essex Institute [1988] *Institutional, Private*
132 Essex St. **Size:** 200
Salem, Massachusetts 01970 **Date Range:** 18th–19th
Ph: (978) 745-1876

Details: Hymnals and tunebooks dating mostly from the first half of the nineteenth century. Thirty eighteenth-century imprints. Some manuscript items.

129. Gordon-Conwell Theological Seminary *Institutional, Private*
Goddard Library **Size:** 500
130 Essex St. **Date Range:** 19th–21st
South Hamilton, Massachusetts 01982 **Lend:** No
Copy: Yes
E-mail: glibrary@gcts.edu
Ph: (978) 646-4074
Fax: (978) 646-4567
Web: www.gordonconwell.edu/library

Details: The Advental Collection includes hymnals of various Protestant denominations, ca. 1800–present, some words-only.

This entry was submitted by Lee Welkley of Berkshire Christian College, Haverhill, Mass., which is part of a consortium with Gordon-Conwell. The collection is housed at Gordon-Conwell.

Denominations: *Advent Christian*

130. Old Stoughton Musical Society
6 Park St.
P.O. Box 794
Stoughton, Massachusetts 02072
Contact: Elizabeth Maraglia, Librarian
Ph: (781) 344-5711

Institutional, Private
Size: 18
Date Range: 18th–19th
Lend: No
Copy: See details below

Details:
Elijah Dunbar Collection (1829–1831);
The Stoughton Musical Society's Centennial Collection of Sacred Music (Boston: Ditson & Co., 1878);
Ancient Harmony Revived ([Maine?], 1848);
Old Hundred Collection of Sacred Music (Boston: printed by Ezra Lincoln, 1824);
French, Jacob. *Harmony of Harmony* (Northampton, Mass.: Andrew Wright, 1802);
Billings, William. *Continental Harmony* (Boston: Thomas and Andrews, 1794) (three copies, incomplete);
Leslie, Benjamin. *The Concert Harmony* (Salem, Mass., 1811);
Kimball, Jacob. *The Essex Harmony* (Exeter, [N.H.], 1800) (two copies);
Billings and Holden. *Collection of Ancient Psalmody* (Boston: Marsh, Capen & Lyon, 1836) (two copies);
The Village Harmony or Youth's Assistant to Sacred Musick (Newburyport, [Mass.]: E. Little & Co, 1815).

The Dunbar books are in better condition than the rest and may be copied at a price. There are newer copies of the society's *Centennial Collection of Sacred Music* and these may be copied as well.

The society archives are not available to the public.

131. Old Sturbridge Village
Research Library
One Old Sturbridge Village Rd.
Sturbridge, Massachusetts 01566
Contact: Colleen Couture, Librarian
Ph: (508) 347-0232
Fax: (508) 347-0295
E-mail: osv@osv.org
Web: www.osv.org

Institutional, Private
Size: 340
Date Range: 1790–1840
Lend: No
Copy: See details below

Details: 340 hymnals and tunebooks; some manuscripts as well. Dates covered: 1790–1840, mostly nineteenth century.

Open to researchers Monday–Friday 9 a.m.–5 p.m. Depending on use and condition of the book, library reserves the right to refuse any copying.

132. Old Colony Historical Society
Hurley Library
66 Church Green
Taunton, Massachusetts 02780
Contact: Greta Smith, Library Assistant
Ph: (508) 822-1622

Institutional, Private
Size: 200
Date Range: 18th–early 20th
Lend: No
Copy: Yes

Details: The collection is uncataloged. Fifty of the eighteenth-century items have Boston or Worcester imprints. The collection includes fifty early-nineteenth-century tunebooks, including *Sacred Harp;* the balance dates from 1850 through 1900.

Open to visitors and researchers Tuesday–Saturday 10 a.m.–4 p.m.

133. Williams College
Archives and Special Collections
Stetson Hall
Williamstown, Massachusetts 01267
Contact: Archivist/ Special Collections Librarian

Institutional, Private
Size: 30
Date Range: 19th
Lend: See details below
Copy: See details below

Ph: (413) 597-2568
Fax: (413) 597-3931
E-mail: archives@williams.edu
Web: www.williams.edu/library/archives
Catalog: francis.williams.edu

Details: Shaker Collection: Material is noncirculating but may be loaned for special exhibitions. Photocopying will be determined by the archives' staff and is dependent upon the condition of the item.

Denominations: *Shaker*

134. American Antiquarian Society
185 Salisbury St.
Worcester, Massachusetts 01609
Contact: Head of Readers' Services
Ph: (508) 755-5221
Fax: (508) 753-3311
E-mail: library@mwa.org
Web: www.americanantiquarian.org/hymnals.htm

Institutional, Private
Size: 8,300
Date Range: 17th–19th
Lend: No
Copy: See details below

Details: Hymnals are found in the Bishop Robert W. Peach Collection and Frank J. Metcalf Collection.

Please see the website for details on use of the library and for an overview of the hymnal collection.

Michigan

135. University of Michigan
Special Collections Library
Hatcher Graduate Library
Ann Arbor, Michigan 48109
Contact: Head, Special Collections Library
Ph: (734) 764-9377
Fax: (734) 764-9368
E-mail: special.collections@umich.edu
Web: www.lib.umich.edu/spec-coll
Catalog: See website

Institutional, Public
Size: 500
Date Range: 15th–19th
Lend: See details below
Copy: See details below

Details: Hymnals spread among the Special Collections Library, the Music Library, and the Clements Library of Americana (see Clements entry). Materials from the Special Collections and Clements libraries do not circulate.

Collections include about 500 cataloged hymnals and tunebooks; texts on hymnology. About 100 in German (from 1760), and 30 in Latin. Most are nineteenth-century American imprints.

Photocopy decisions are based on whether the material will be damaged by copying.

Denominations: *Shaker*

136. University of Michigan
William L. Clements Library
909 S. University Ave.
Ann Arbor, Michigan 48109-1190
Contact: Book Division Curator
Ph: (734) 764-2347
Fax: (734) 647-0716
E-mail: books.clements@umich.edu
Web: www.clements.umich.edu

Institutional, Public
Size: 230
Date Range: 18th–19th
Lend: No
Copy: See details below

Details: About 200 early American and German hymnals; 31 volumes of hymnology pre-1821.

Limited copying (the library does not do whole-book copying).

137. Andrews University
Adventist Heritage Center
James White Library
Berrien Springs, Michigan 49104
Contact: Curator
Ph: (616) 471-3274
Fax: (616) 471-2646
E-mail: ahc@andrews.edu
Web: www.andrews.edu/library

Institutional, Private
Size: 150
Date Range: 19th–20th
Lend: No
Copy: See details below

Details: Franklin E. Belden Songbook Collection: Collection of songbooks from the library of Belden, prominent songwriter from the last quarter of the nineteenth century and first part of the twentieth. Wide range of titles and sources. Not cataloged.

Also Seventh-day Adventist Hymn and Songbook Collection. About 150 cataloged hymnals, a few words-only, dating from 1843. Emphasis on gospel songs. Some African, Asian, European, and South American.

Some photocopy restrictions. Open to visitors and researchers Monday–Thursday 9 a.m.–9 p.m., Friday 9 a.m.–1 p.m., Sunday 1–9 p.m.

Denominations: *Seventh-day Adventist*

138. Detroit Public Library
Music & Performing Arts Dept.
5201 Woodward Ave.
Detroit, Michigan 48202
Contact: Ellen Simmons, Manager
Ph: (313) 833-1460
E-mail: esimmon@detroit.lib.mi.us
Web: www.detroit.lib.mi.us
Catalog: See website

Institutional, Public
Size: 630
Date Range: 19th–21st
Lend: See details below
Copy: See details below

Details: Approximately 500 cataloged hymnals, and the Mary Louise Handley Collection of 130 uncataloged hymnals.

Will loan circulating items. Will copy items in public domain.

139. Western Theological Seminary
Beardslee Library
101 E. 13th St.
Holland, Michigan 49423
Contact: Paul M. Smith, Director
Ph: (616) 392-8555
Fax: (616) 392-8880
E-mail: paul.smith@westernsem.org
Web: www.westernsem.org/library

Institutional, Private
Size: 150
Date Range: 19th–20th
Lend: See details below
Copy: See details below

Details: Collection includes some hymnals in Dutch and other languages. Hymnals from Reformed Church in America and other Reformed denominations.

Lending possible for items in the circulating collection. Copying possible for items in good physical condition. Charges may apply to both.

Denominations: *Presbyterian, Reformed, Reformed Church in America*

140. Manistee County Historical Museum [1988]
425 River St.
Manistee, Michigan 49660
Ph: (231) 723-5531

Institutional, Private
Size: 50
Date Range: 1875–1925

Details: Includes hymnals in German and Polish.

Minnesota

141. Wright County Historical Society
2001 Hwy 25 N.
Buffalo, Minnesota 55313
Contact: Betty Dircks, Archivist
Ph: (763) 682-7323
Fax: (763) 682-8945
E-mail: wchsmg@visi.com

Institutional, Public
Size: 75
Date Range: 1900–present
Lend: No

Details: About seventy-five uncataloged Lutheran hymnals, 1900–present. Some in Swedish.

Denominations: *Lutheran*

142. Bethany Lutheran Theological Seminary
Library
6 Browns Ct.
Mankato, Minnesota 56001
Contact: Gaylin Schmeling, President

Institutional, Private
Size: 800
Date Range: 16th–20th
Lend: See details below
Copy: See details below

Ph: (507) 344-7354
E-mail: gschmeli@blc.edu
Web: www.blc.edu/library
Catalog: See website

Details: Hymnals gathered by Rev. Markus F. Wiese, 1842–1927, are the core of the 800 volumes of the uncataloged collection. Classified by language, emphasis is on Norwegian and Danish. Mostly American Lutheran synods are represented. Microfiche title page display is available.

Open Monday–Friday 8 a.m.–5 p.m., Saturday 8 a.m.–noon (no Saturday hours in summer). Will photocopy but not mail books.

Denominations: *Lutheran*

143. Norman P. Heitz
3209 Garfield Ave.
Minneapolis, Minnesota 55408
Ph: (612) 825-7579
E-mail: normanheitz@juno.com

Individual
Size: 175
Date Range: late 18th–20th
Lend: No
Copy: Yes

Details: Multiple copies of American Lutheran hymnals, late-twentieth-century, especially Evangelical Lutheran Church in America (ELCA); 175 uncataloged miscellaneous hymnals; would exchange.

Denominations: *Evangelical Lutheran Church in America*

144. Minneapolis Public Library
Art/Music/Video Department
300 Nicollet Mall
Minneapolis, Minnesota 55401
Contact: Librarian
Ph: (612) 630-6330
Fax: (612) 630-6210
E-mail: Art/Music/Video@mplib.org
Web: www.mplib.org

Institutional, Public
Size: 1,000
Date Range: 19th–20th
Lend: Yes
Copy: No

Details: The library has 1,000 hymnals, tunebooks, and books on hymnody dating from the nineteenth and twentieth centuries.

145. United Methodist Church
Minnesota Conference Archives
122 W. Franklin Ave., Suite 400
Minneapolis, Minnesota 55404
Contact: Thelma Boeder, Archivist
Ph: (612) 870-0058
Fax: (612) 870-1260
E-mail: thelma.boeder@mnumc.org
Web: www.mnumc.org

Institutional, Private
Size: 150
Date Range: 19th–20th
Lend: No
Copy: Yes

Details: United Methodist Church and antecedents (Methodist Episcopal, Methodist Church, Evangelical Church, United Brethren in Christ, Evangelical United Brethren). Mostly English language, some German, Norwegian, and Swedish.

Denominations: *Evangelical Church, Evangelical United Brethren, Methodist Church, Methodist Episcopal, United Brethren in Christ, United Methodist*

146. University of Minnesota
Music Library
2106 4th St.
Minneapolis, Minnesota 55455
Contact: Music Librarian
Ph: (612) 624-8552
E-mail: musiclib@tc.umn.edu
Web: music.lib.umn.edu
Catalog: See website

Institutional, Public
Size: 500
Date Range: 18th–20th
Lend: Yes
Copy: Yes

Details: The library has 107 tunebooks (1794–1859) and 386 hymnals (1880–1920). The collection includes 200 hymnals in European languages, but published in the midwestern United States.

Denominations: *Catholic*

147. St. Olaf College [1988]
Norwegian American Historical Association

Institutional, Private
Size: 700

Rolvaag Memorial Library
1510 St. Olaf Ave.
Northfield, Minnesota 55057-1097
Ph: (507) 646-3221
E-mail: naha@stolaf.edu
Web: www.naha.stolaf.edu

Details: About 700 cataloged hymnals. Words-only hymnals include 114 Norwegian or Danish, 40 German, 12 Swedish, 6 Latin, and 60 English. Hymnals with music include 200 in English, 114 Norwegian or Danish, 10 German, and 9 Swedish. Primarily Lutheran, but some other denominations.

Denominations: *Lutheran*

148. Bethel Theological Seminary [1988]
Carl H. Lundquist Library
3949 Bethel Dr.
St. Paul, Minnesota 55112
Ph: (651) 638-6184
Web: www.bethel.edu/library.htm

Institutional, Private
Size: 500
Date Range: 1628–1940

Details: The library has 500 hymnals representing many denominations; 200 are in Swedish. Some are words-only.

149. Concordia University
Buenger Memorial Library
275 N. Syndicate St.
St. Paul, Minnesota 55110
Contact: Charlotte Knoche, Reference Librarian
Ph: (651) 641-8241
Fax: (651) 659-0207
E-mail: knoche@csp.edu
Web: www.csp.edu/virtuallibrary
Catalog: clicnet.clic.edu/search

Institutional, Private
Size: 800
Date Range: 19th–20th
Lend: See details below
Copy: See details below

Details: The Arthur Billings Hunt Hymnology Collection was obtained from Macalester College, St. Paul, Minn. Areas emphasized include German Lutheran, gospel, and tunebooks.

Would be happy to lend or copy some materials, unless materials are too fragile. Patron may need to help with costs of copying, depending on quantity desired.

Denominations: *Lutheran Church–Missouri Synod*

150. Luther Seminary
Library
2481 Como Ave.
St. Paul, Minnesota 55108
Contact: Bruce Eldevik,
Reference Librarian
Ph: (651) 641-3226
Fax: (651) 641-3280
E-mail: beldevik@luthersem.edu
Web: www.luthersem.edu/library
Catalog: ruth.luthersem.edu

Institutional, Private
Size: 1,400
Date Range: 16th–20th
Lend: See details below
Copy: Yes

Details: The Carl Doving Hymn Collection is a collection of hymnbooks in many different languages and dialects; there are 43 languages and dialects from Europe, 93 from Asia, 120 from Africa, 24 from America, 2 from Australia, 1 from New Zealand, 42 from Oceania, and many more. Once housed at Luther College, the collection was placed on permanent loan to Luther Seminary in the 1950s. In 1997, Luther College transferred ownership of the collection to the seminary. It is now housed as one of the seminary's special collections in its climate-controlled Rare Book Room. Approximately 1,500 volumes ranging in date from the mid-1650s to the early 1900s. The collection is strong in hymnody as it developed in overseas missions, particularly in the nineteenth and twentieth centuries. Lutheranism is especially strong, as witnessed through the publications of their world mission societies, but other denominational world mission activities are also well represented. Scandinavian hymnals and psalters from the immigration period of the nineteenth century are particularly strong in the general collection. The library has no personal papers or other manuscript collections relevant to hymnody, but many of the hymnals in the Doving Collection contain extensive notes in Doving's hand detailing how the hymnal was obtained as well other annotations related to the item.

The Doving Collection is supplemented by materials housed in the Special Collections Department: facsimile editions of early Luther hymnals and microfilmed copies of Lutheran and Reformed hymnals of the sixteenth and seventeenth centuries from the Continent and Scandinavian countries. In addition, there are examples of Books of Common Prayer and Sternhold/Hopkins's *The Whole Book of Psalms,* in early and subsequent editions. Hymnals and psalters from the British Isles and the Americas of the eighteenth and nineteenth centuries are included, as are hymnals and psalmbooks from the North American Lutheran traditions. The general collection houses all of the library's denominational hymnals from the twentieth century. New titles are added in all areas regularly. The Doving Collection is currently accessible through the library's public-access catalog, electronically through the website, and in-house through a separate shelflist located in the Rare Book Room. Items in the collection are identified as such in a local notes field.

Titles from the Doving Collection do not circulate. Special Collections hours are Monday–Friday, 8 a.m.–5 p.m. Microfilm materials are available through interlibrary loan.

Denominations: *Lutheran, Reformed*

151. Minnesota Historical Society [1988]
345 W. Kellogg Blvd.
St. Paul, Minnesota 55102-1906
Ph: (651) 296-2143
Web: www.mnhs.org/library

Institutional, Private
Size: 400
Date Range: 19th–early 20th

Details: About 350–400 cataloged hymnals of which 150 are in Swedish, 40 in Norwegian, 50 in Chippewa or Dakota. Mid-nineteenth to early twentieth centuries.

152. Gustavus Adolphus College [1988]

Institutional, Private
Size: 500

Folke Bernadotte Library
800 W. College Ave.
St. Peter, Minnesota 56082
Contact: Archivist
Ph: (507) 933-7572
Web: oncampus.gustavus.edu/oncampus/academics/library

Date Range: 19th–20th

Details: The library has 111 cataloged hymnals with strong emphasis on Swedish Lutheran items. Supplemented by works on liturgics and history of hymns.

There are also 375 cataloged hymnals from 1859 to 1958 (52 words-only) with over 200 in Swedish. Also some in English, German, and Norwegian. Eleven items numerically noted for psalmodikon.

Denominations: *Lutheran*

153. Carver County Historical Society
Library
555 W. First St.
Waconia, Minnesota 55387
Contact: Curator
Ph: (952) 442-4234
Fax: (952) 442-3025
E-mail: historical@co.carver.mn.us
Web: www.carvercountyhistoricalsociety.org

Institutional, Public
Size: 100
Date Range: 19th–20th
Lend: See details below
Copy: Yes

Details: Collection is uncataloged. Cataloging is scheduled for late 2002, after which the collection will be available for research. Will consider loans to other institutions on a case-by-case basis.

Denominations: *Augustana Synod, Lutheran Church–Missouri Synod, Moravian*

Mississippi

154. William Carey College
Rouse Library
498 Tuscan Ave.
Hattiesburg, Mississippi 39401

Institutional, Private
Size: 500
Date Range: 20th
Lend: No

Contact: Dr. Eugene Winters, Winters School of Music
Copy: No
Ph: (601) 582-6182
Fax: (601) 582-6171
E-mail: gwinters@wmcarey.edu
Web: www.wmcarey.edu

Details: Clarence Dickinson Collection: 500 partly cataloged American hymnals, plus 300 volumes of church music.

Open to visitors and researchers by appointment.

Denominations: *Baptist*

Missouri

155. Community of Christ
Institutional, Public
Library
1001 W. Walnut
Independence, Missouri 64050
Contact: Suzanne McDonald, Librarian
Size: 100
Date Range: 19th–20th
Lend: No
Copy: Yes
Ph: (816) 833-1000
Fax: (816) 521-3089
E-mail: smcdonald@cofchrist.org
Web: www.cofchrist.org/templeschool/library
Catalog: See website

Details: About 100 hymnals dating from 1830. Some are words-only.

Denominations: *Community of Christ*

156. R. Duane Stephens
Individual
100 N. Pleasant
Independence, Missouri 64050
Ph: (816) 252-6662
Fax: (816) 252-3300
E-mail: duaneind@swbell.net
Size: 1,900
Date Range: 18th–20th
Lend: No
Copy: Yes

Details: Official hymnals of most major denominations, church school hymnals, independent publishers, and many handbooks or companions to hymnals.

Denominations: *Baptist, Community of Christ, Methodist, Presbyterian*

157. Ken Bible
103 E. 127th St.
Kansas City, Missouri 64145
Ph: (816) 942-8285
Fax: (816) 943-9337
E-mail: LNW@tfs.net

Individual
Size: 30
Date Range: 18th–20th
Lend: No
Copy: See details below

Details: A few dozen German hymnals from the eighteenth, nineteenth, and twentieth centuries. Highlights include:
Gregor, Christian, ed. *Gesangbuch zum Gebrauch der evangelischen Brudergemeinen* (Barby, Germany: Lorenz Friedrich Spellenberg, 1778);
Gerhardt, Paulus. *Geistliche Lieder* (Philadelphia, Pa., 1890);
Das Kleine Davidische Psalterspiel (Philadelphia, Pa.: G. Mentz und Sohn) 1833;
Erbauliche Lieder-Sammlung. (Germantaun, Pa.: gedruckt bey Michael Billmeyer, 1803). [For Evangelical Lutheran Ministerium of Pennsylvania];
Unpartheyisches Gesangbuch (Lancaster: Johann Bar, 1820).

Photocopying done only for truly pressing research needs.

Denominations: *Evangelical Lutheran Ministerium of Pennsylvania, Mennonite, Moravian*

158. University of Missouri-Kansas City [1988]
University Libraries
5100 Rockhill Rd.
Kansas City, Missouri 64110
Ph: (816) 235-1534
Web: www.umkc.edu/lib

Institutional, Public
Size: 1,000

Details: Over 1,000 partly cataloged American hymnals of various denominations.

159. William Jewell College
Institutional, Private
Charles F. Curry Library
500 College Hill
Box 1097
Liberty, Missouri 64068
Contact: Bonnie Knauss, Special Collections Librarian
Ph: (816) 781-7700
Fax: (816) 415-5021
E-mail: knaussb@william.jewell.edu
Web: www.jewell.edu/academics/curry/library

Size: 300
Date Range: 19th
Lend: No
Copy: See details below

Details: Charles Haddon Spurgeon Collection: Mostly nineteenth-century British and American hymnals and shape-note tunebooks. These items are not included in the online catalog.

Will copy if condition of book allows. Collection open Monday–Friday 8 a.m.–5 p.m., or by appointment.

***Denominations:** Baptist*

160. William Jewell College
Institutional, Private
Partee Center for Baptist Historical Studies
500 College Hill
Box 1023
Liberty, Missouri 64068
Contact: Angela N. Stiffler, Archival Director
Ph: (816) 781-7700
E-mail: stifflera@william.jewell.edu
Web:
www.jewell.edu/academics/curry/Library/partee/partee.html

Size: 75
Date Range: 19th–20th
Lend: No
Copy: Yes

Details: Collection includes nineteenth- and twentieth-century hymnals, and some shape-note items.

Open Monday–Friday by appointment. Will copy if condition allows.

Denominations: *Baptist*

161. John W. Baker
2727 Catalina Ave.
Springfield, Missouri 65804
Ph: (417) 882-4166
E-mail: jnanbak@atlascomm.net

Individual
Size: 500
Date Range: late 19th–20th
Lend: Yes
Copy: Yes

Details: Several words-only hymnals, including small pocket-size; some reprints of oblong singing school books; several from the nineteenth through early twentieth century; leans toward gospel, evangelistic; many paperback books from denominations, revival promotion, private printing, etc.; large number of texts having to do with hymnology (history, hymn stories, etc.); several hymnals in languages other than English.

Denominations: *Baptist*

162. Concordia Historical Institute
801 DeMun Ave.
St. Louis, Missouri 63105
Contact: Associate Director for Archives & Library
Ph: (314) 505-7900
Fax: (314) 505-7901
E-mail: chi@chi.lcms.org
Web: chi.lcms.org
Catalog: See website

Institutional, Private
Size: 1,000
Date Range: 17th–20th
Lend: No
Copy: Yes

Details: Hymnals of Lutheran church bodies of North America and of European antecedents, and hymnals produced for Lutheran mission activity throughout the world. The institute also has some manuscripts and personal papers related to the preparation and publishing of hymnals in the Lutheran Church–Missouri Synod. See also Concordia Seminary entry.

Denominations: *Lutheran, Lutheran Church–Missouri Synod*

163. Concordia Seminary
Library
801 De Mun Ave.
St. Louis, Missouri 63105
Contact: David O. Berger, Director
Ph: (314) 505-7040
Fax: (314) 505-7046
E-mail: bergerd@csl.edu
Web: www.csl.edu/library
Catalog: See website

Institutional, Private
Size: 300
Date Range: 16th–present
Lend: See details below
Copy: See details below

Details: The Martens Collection consists of 108 psalters and hymnals. Most are American publications from the eighteenth and nineteenth centuries; a smaller number are German publications from the same period. Hymnals in the regular cataloged collection consist primarily of several hundred Lutheran hymnals from the sixteenth century to the present, many from specific regions of Germany following the Reformation; and German hymnals published in the United States, primarily by the Lutheran Church–Missouri Synod and its predecessor bodies. The remainder of the cataloged collection (about 200 volumes) is eclectic and representative. In addition to nondenominational publications, it includes a broad representation of denominational hymnals from the United States, mostly from the late nineteenth through the late twentieth century. Consists of mostly Lutheran and some Protestant and Catholic hymnals. The library attempts to have a comprehensive collection of Lutheran hymnals. Beyond that, the focus is on providing a broad representation of current and recent hymnals of other U.S. denominations.

Approximately 200 of the oldest German hymnals, still in Dewey classification, are not in the online catalog but are accessible onsite in the card catalog. No personal papers, although there are some historical documents relating to the preparation of *The Lutheran Hymnal* and *Lutheran Worship*.

Copying and lending subject to condition and rarity of item.

Denominations: *Catholic, Lutheran, Lutheran Church–Missouri Synod, nondenominational*

164. The Lutheran Church–Missouri Synod
Central Library
LCMS International Center
1333 S. Kirkwood Rd.
St. Louis, Missouri 63122
Contact: Wendi Adams
Ph: (314) 965-9000
Fax: (314) 822-8307
E-mail: wendi.adams@lcms.org
Catalog: www.csl.edu/library/catalog.htm

Institutional, Private
Size: 1,100
Date Range: 19th–21st
Lend: See details below
Copy: See details below

Details: Hymnals dating from 1800 to 1940. Some in German and Scandinavian languages; also volumes on hymnology.

Copying and lending is done according to established patron guidelines.

Denominations: *Lutheran Church–Missouri Synod*

165. Missouri Historical Society
Library
P.O. Box 11940
225 S. Skinker Blvd.
St. Louis, Missouri 63112-0040
Contact: Librarian
Ph: (314) 746-4500
Fax: (314) 746-4548
E-mail: library@mohistory.org
Web: www.mohistory.org/LRC.html
Catalog: mohistory.library.net

Institutional, Private
Size: 100
Date Range: 19th–20th
Lend: See details below
Copy: See details below

Details: Mostly nineteenth-century, many German hymnals, tunebooks, and songbooks. Ten copies of Allen Carden, *Missouri Harmony* (1820–1857), and one John B. Seat, *St. Louis Harmony* (Cincinnati: Lodge & L'Hommedieu, 1831). Most others in collection are uncataloged; approximately six boxes of "Hymnals and Songsters."

Noncirculating library, free and open to public who register on initial visit. Staff makes copies if items are not too fragile. Will loan to other museums for exhibit.

166. Washington University
Gaylord Music Library
6500 Forsyth Blvd.
St. Louis, Missouri 63130
Contact: Music Librarian
Ph: (314) 935-5529
Fax: (314) 935-4263
E-mail: music@library.wustl.edu
Web: library.wustl.edu/units/music
Catalog: catalog.wustl.edu

Institutional, Private
Size: 700
Date Range: 18th–20th
Lend: See details below
Copy: See details below

Details: Highlights include 40 Lowell Mason items, 67 St. Louis imprints, 10 eighteenth-century items, 273 nineteenth-century items, and 210 non-English items.

Modern editions include Eastern Church (Slavic, Greek, Russian), Roman Catholic, German, Scottish, Tamil, and English (largely Protestant).

Pre-1900 imprints are located in Special Collections and are available Monday–Friday 9 a.m.–5 p.m.

Denominations: *Catholic, Orthodox*

Nebraska

167. Nebraska United Methodist Annual Conference
United Methodist Historical Center
5000 St. Paul Ave.
P.O. Box 4553
Lincoln, Nebraska 68504
Contact: Director/Curator
Ph: (402) 465-2175
E-mail: nebrumchc@yahoo.com
Web: www.umcneb.org/html/history.html

Institutional, Private
Size: 454
Date Range: 18th–21st
Lend: No
Copy: Yes

Details: Mostly United Methodist and its predecessors, including 25 in German, and a few in Chinese, Danish, Japanese, and Swedish. Also, evangelistic, Sunday school, children's, men's, and special occasions. There are 307 cataloged items, and 147 uncataloged.

Open to researchers and visitors Tuesday, Wednesday, Thursday.

Denominations: *Evangelical Church, Evangelical United Brethren, Methodist Church, Methodist Episcopal, United Brethren in Christ, United Methodist*

New Hampshire

168. Canterbury Shaker Village [1988]
288 Shaker Rd.
Canterbury, New Hampshire 03224
Ph: (603) 783-9511 or (866) 783-9511
Web: www.shakers.org

Institutional, Private
Size: 80
Date Range: 19th–20th

Details: The collection includes forty manuscript songbooks dating from the late nineteenth century. Collection also includes works by Dorothy Durgin (d. 1898).

Denominations: *Shaker*

169. New Hampshire Historical Society
Tuck Library
30 Park St.
Concord, New Hampshire 03301
Contact: William Copeley
Ph: (603) 225-3381
Fax: (603) 224-0463
E-mail: bcopeley@nhhistory.org
Web: www.nhhistory.org/library.html
Catalog: See website

Institutional, Private
Size: 100
Date Range: 18th–19th
Lend: No
Copy: Yes

Details: Open year-round Tuesday–Saturday 9:30 a.m.–5:00 p.m. $6 per day user fee for nonmembers. Copies 25¢ per page.

Denominations: *Baptist, Congregational, Shaker*

170. Dartmouth College
Paddock Music Library
6187 Hopkins Center
Hanover, New Hampshire 03755
Contact: Reference Librarian
Ph: (603) 646-3234
Fax: (603) 646-1219
E-mail: Paddock.Music.Library@Dartmouth.edu
Web: www.dartmouth.edu/~paddock
Catalog: inno.dartmouth.edu

Institutional, Private
Size: 477
Date Range: 18th–20th
Lend: See details below
Copy: See details below

Details: The library has 477 cataloged hymnals, including some hymnological items. Mostly in English, but 54 German, also some French, Greek, Hebrew, and Latin. From late eighteenth century, including much material from Isaiah Thomas, presented in 1819, including tunebooks. Also 35 nineteenth-century tunebooks.

Open to visitors and researchers Monday–Thursday 8 a.m.–10 p.m., Friday 8 a.m.–5 p.m., Saturday 1–5 p.m., Sunday 1–10 p.m. Will photocopy and send via interlibrary loan. Will consider exhange.

171. Thomas and Agnes Ellis
P.O. Box 552
Henniker, New Hampshire 03242
Ph: (603) 428-3464

Individual
Size: 550
Date Range: 19th–ca.1970
Copy: No

Details: Mostly Protestant and nondenominational. A few Catholic, a few His Way. Some school music books with hymns; a few stories of hymns; a few country and western gospel. One in Welsh, a few in German, Swedish, and French (Canadian).

Denominations: *Catholic, nondenominational*

172. Manchester City Library
Art/Music Rooms
405 Pine St.
Manchester, New Hampshire

Institutional, Public
Size: 35
Date Range: 19th–20th
Lend: Yes

03104
Contact: Beverly M. White, Librarian
Ph: (603) 624-6550
Fax: (603) 624-6559
E-mail: bwhite@ci.manchester.nh.us
Web: www.manchester.lib.nh.us
Catalog: See website

Copy: Yes

Details: Hymnals and songbooks dating from the nineteenth and twentieth centuries.

New Jersey

173. Drew University
Library
36 Madison Ave.
Madison, New Jersey 07940
Contact: See below
Ph: See below
Fax: (973) 408-3770
E-mail: See below
Web: www.depts.drew.edu/lib
Catalog: See website

Institutional, Private
Size: See below
Date Range: 17th–present
Lend: See details below
Copy: See details below

Details: The cornerstone of Drew University's collection of 7,000 hymnals is a group of 700 Methodist and denominational hymnals acquired in 1868 from David Creamer (1812–1887), a Baltimore businessman, prominent Methodist layman, and author of the first American commentary on Wesleyan hymns, *Methodist Hymnology* (New York, 1848). Creamer's collection is the largest and earliest (pre–Civil War) collection of hymnody in the United States which is still intact. Many of the volumes contain his extensive annotations regarding variant editions and dates, the music sources and publishing histories of earlier editions, and the identification of unsigned texts. During the last century, the hymnology collection has grown to over 7,000 volumes, spanning nearly 400 years. More than twenty-five countries and twenty languages are represented, as well as more than twenty-five Methodist churches (American and British) and numerous other denominations and interest groups.

There are 4,000 Methodist hymnals, housed in the Methodist Center, which date from the early nineteenth century to the present. Housed in the main library are about 3,000 non-Methodist hymnals, ranging in date from 1603 to the present. Gifts and purchases of all Methodist materials are actively pursued. No new purchases are made for non-Methodist items; gifts are evaluated. Although the Methodist hymnals are uncataloged, a comprehensive finding aid exists in the form of nine notebooks containing photocopies of the title page of each volume. These are arranged by country, denomination, date, and language. They may be consulted in the Methodist Center. Cataloging of the non-Methodist hymnals is ongoing. About 1,500 items (including 1,000 up to the year 1868) are available through the online catalog.

Only circulating volumes in our main library stacks are available for lending via interlibrary loan. Limited in-house photocopying available. Volumes may or may not be copied depending upon condition of the particular volume.

For information on the Creamer Collection, contact Lessie Culmer-Nier, Head of Cataloging, (973) 408-3477, lculmern@drew.edu. For information on the Methodist Collection, contact Jocelyne Rubinetti, Methodist Library Associate, (973) 408-3590, jrubinet@drew.edu.

Denominations: *Methodist*

174. New Brunswick Theological Seminary
Gardner A. Sage Library
21 Seminary Place
New Brunswick, New Jersey 08901
Contact: Renee House, Director
Ph: (201) 247-5243
E-mail: rsh@nbts.edu
Web: www.nbts.edu

Institutional, Private
Size: 500
Date Range: 16th–present
Lend: See details below
Copy: Yes

Details: Approximately 500 hymnals cataloged, sixteenth century–present, many duplicates. Special collection of Reformed Church in America hymnals, large collection of metrical psalms, hymnals of most mainline Protestant denominations. Hymnals/psalters in Dutch, French, Gaelic, German, and Latin.

Will photocopy and interlibrary loan. Open Monday–Thursday 10 a.m.–10 p.m., Friday 10 a.m.–5 p.m., Saturday 11 a.m.–9 p.m. Summer: Monday–Friday 10 a.m.–5 p.m.

Denominations: *Reformed Church in America*

175. Princeton Theological Seminary
Library
Princeton, New Jersey 08542
Contact: Special Collections Librarian
Ph: (609) 497-7940
Web: www.ptsem.edu/grow/library.htm

Institutional, Private
Size: 12,000
Date Range: 18th–20th
Lend: No

Details: Benson Collection of Hymnology: This collection consists of approximately 12,000 volumes of hymnals and hymnology. The original 9,000 volumes were willed to the seminary by Louis FitzGerald Benson at his death in 1930. Benson was the editor of the 1895 and 1911 Presbyterian hymnals, the author of *The English Hymn* (New York: Hodder & Stoughton, G. H. Doran, 1915). He also left an endowment to maintain and upgrade the collection. The collection is comprehensive in nature and includes a number of exceptionally rare items, among which are first editions of Watts's *Hymns and Spiritual Songs* and his *Psalms of David Imitated in the Language of the New Testament*. Both copies are autographed. There is a wealth of British and American imprints and significant numbers of Greek, Latin, European, Asian, and Native American hymnals. About 1,000 titles were added from the Presbyterian Historical Society's holdings in 1994. Regular purchases of virtually all American hymnals and hymnological works and as many as possible from other countries and in languages other than English are added regularly. The seminary's library holdings, including all special collections, may be accessed via the seminary's web page.

Denominations: *Presbyterian*

176. Princeton University [1988]
Princeton Collections of Western Americana
One Washington Rd.
Princeton, New Jersey 08544
Contact: Curator
Ph: (609) 258-6156
Fax: (609) 258-2324
E-mail: west@princeton.edu
Web: www.princeton.edu/~rbsc/department/western

Institutional, Private
Size: 100
Date Range: 19th

Details: About 100 cataloged Mormon hymnals, mostly nineteenth-century.

Denominations: *Church of Jesus Christ of Latter-day Saints*

177. Gertrude Suppe
35 Hamilton Ave.
Princeton, New Jersey 08542
Ph: (609) 924-6509
E-mail: gcsuppe@aol.com

Individual
Size: 600
Date Range: 20th
Lend: No
Copy: Yes

Details: The collection includes bound hymnals, *cancioneros,** catalogs, periodicals, correspondence, cassette tapes (mostly nonprofessional), phonograph records, etc. Languages: Spanish, Portuguese. Database with information on 600 hymnals and *cancioneros,* and at least 15,000 individual hymns. Much more not yet entered. Detailed description and projected eventual disposition of collection. Mostly dating from post–Vatican II.

**Cancioneros* are small paperback booklets in Spanish. There are usually ten to thirty songs in one volume, often privately or locally printed.

Denominations: *Catholic, United Methodist*

178. Westminster Choir College of Rider University
Talbott Library
101 Walnut Ln.
Princeton, New Jersey 08540

Institutional, Private
Size: 3,500
Date Range: 15th–21st
Lend: See details below
Copy: See details below

Contact: Nancy Wicklund,
Special Collections Librarian
Ph: (609) 921-7100
Fax: (609) 497-0243
E-mail: wicklund@rider.edu
Web: library.rider.edu/talbott/specialcollections.html
Catalog: library.rider.edu/catalog.htm

Details:
Erik Routley Collection of Books & Hymnals;
Erik Routley Papers;
Thomas Tiplady Collection;
Winfred Douglas/Walter Williams Collection of Liturgical & Choral Music;
Lee Hastings Bristol, Jr. Hymnals (incorporated into general holdings);
Hymnal 1982 Working Papers.

Circulating items available on interlibrary loan. For Special Collections descriptions and access, see the library's website. See also Nancy Wicklund, "The Erik Routley Collection of Books and Hymnals at Talbott Library, Westminster Choir College of Rider University." *The Hymn* 53, no. 4 (October 2002): 46–49.

Denominations: *Anglican, Episcopal*

New York

179. New York State Library [1988] *Institutional, Public*
Cultural Education Center
Date Range: 19th
Empire State Plaza
Albany, New York 12230
Ph: (518) 474-5355
Web: www.nysl.nysed.gov

Details: Hymnals and other choral music, both published and manuscript. Includes nine Shaker hymnals.

Denominations: *Shaker*

180. Brooklyn Public Library [1988] *Institutional, Public*
Size: 300

Central Library, Art and Music Division
Grand Army Plaza
Brooklyn, New York 11238
Ph: (718) 230-2100
Web: www.brooklynpubliclibrary.org

Date Range: 1820–present

Details: The library has 300 volumes of songbooks and hymnals, dating from 1820.

181. **Buffalo & Erie County Public Library**
1 Lafayette Sq.
Buffalo, New York 14203
Contact: Raya Then
Ph: (716) 858-7119
Fax: (716) 858-8087
E-mail: thenr@buffalolib.org
Web: www.buffalolib.org
Catalog: See website

Institutional, Public
Size: 770
Date Range: 1820–20th
Lend: Yes
Copy: Yes

Details: About 770 cataloged hymnals from 1820. Many denominations, including Shaker. Some foreign languages, including German. Open to visitors and researchers.

Denominations: *Shaker*

182. **Hamilton College**
Burke Library
198 College Hill Rd.
Clinton, New York 13323
Contact: April Caprak, Library Secretary
Ph: (315) 859-4475
Fax: (315) 859-4578
E-mail: acaprak@hamilton.edu
Web: www.hamilton.edu/library
Catalog: See website

Institutional, Private
Size: 15
Date Range: 19th
Copy: See details below
Lend: No

Details: Fifteen Shaker manuscript hymnals, some in letteral notation. Some include author's signature and community. All are in the noncirculating Rare Book Collection and may be used in the library only by appointment. Depending on condition, copies can be made upon request.

Denominations: *Shaker*

183. Janice T. Woods
6 Frontier Ln.
East Northport, New York 11731
Ph: (631) 368-4836

Individual
Size: 400
Date Range: 18th–21st
Lend: No
Copy: Yes

Details: Methodist hymnals 1845–1989; facsimile of John Wesley's *First Hymn Book: Collection of Psalms and Hymns* (1737). Some earlier Methodist hymnals, published in England.

Several nineteenth-century singing school songbooks. Hymnals of several denominations and languages, including German, Swedish, and Welsh. Twenty-one hymnals are words-only. Some radio artists books: Edward McHugh, L. P. Lehman, Ed McConnell, *Back to the Bible*. Some pocket-size hymnals, words-only. Some books on hymnology.

Denominations: *Methodist, United Methodist*

184. Queens College (CUNY)
Music Library
65-30 Kissena Blvd.
Flushing, New York 11367-0904
Contact: Joseph Ponte, Head
Ph: (718) 997-3901
Fax: (718) 997-3849
E-mail: jponte@qc1.qc.edu
Web: www.qc.edu/Library/mmusic.html
Catalog: libraries.cuny.edu/lib-cpl.htm

Institutional, Public
Size: 100
Date Range: 19th
Lend: No
Copy: Yes

Details: American Sunday school, revival, mission, shape-note, temperance, Lutheran, Methodist, Presbyterian, and Shaker hymnals. Dates mostly from the first half of the nineteenth century.

Denominations: *Lutheran, Methodist, Presbyterian, Shaker*

185. Cornell University
Sidney Cox Library of Music and Dance
Lincoln Hall
Ithaca, New York 14853-4101
Contact: Music Librarian
Ph: (607) 255-4011
Fax: (607) 254-2877
E-mail: musicref@cornell.edu
Web: www.library.cornell.edu/music
Catalog: catalog.library.cornell.edu

Institutional, Private
Size: 120
Date Range: 1788–1921
Lend: No
Copy: See details below

Details: The Harris Hymnal Collection is described in Sander L. Gilman, "German Hymnals in the Harris Hymnal Collection: A Short-Title Check List," *The Cornell Library Journal* 10 (winter 1970): 40–48.

Will make photocopies if material will not be damaged in the process.

Denominations: *Lutheran*

186. Museum Village [1988]
1010 Route 17M
Monroe, New York 10950
Ph: (845) 782-8247
Fax: (845) 782-6432
E-mail: info@museumvillage.org
Web: www.museumvillage.org

Institutional, Private
Size: 45
Date Range: 19th

Details: Hymnals, tunebooks, and songbooks. Includes Little and Smith, *Easy Instructor* (Albany: [inscribed 1821]), and Thomas Hartwell, *The New York & Vermont Collection* (Albany: n.d.).

187. Columbia University
Rare Book and Manuscript Library
535 W. 114th St.
New York, New York 10027
Contact: Director
Ph: (212) 854-5153

Institutional, Private
Size: 500
Date Range: 16th–20th
Lend: No
Copy: See details below

Fax: (212) 854-1365
E-mail: rarebooks@libraries.cul.columbia.edu
Web: www.columbia.edu/cu/lweb/indiv/rare

Details: The Hunt-Berol Collection, formed by Arthur Billings Hunt, contains some 3,000 volumes of mostly American and English music books of the sixteenth–twentieth (mostly eighteenth and nineteenth) centuries. It includes over 500 volumes of sacred music, particularly eighteenth- and nineteenth-century British and American hymnology. The collection is not cataloged; access is by in-house card files and lists. In a related collection are 12 manuscripts and printed books from the Ephrata Cloister.

Please contact the library about access policies. Material does not circulate, but microfilming is possible.

Denominations: *German Seventh Day Baptist*

188. New York Historical Society
170 Central Park West
New York, New York 10024
Contact: Margaret Heilbrun, Library Director
Ph: (212) 873-3400
Web: www.nyhistory.org

Institutional, Private
Size: 700
Date Range: 18th–early 19th
Lend: No
Copy: See details below

Details: The society has 700 tunebooks and hymnals dating from the late eighteenth century. Copies from stable items only, at discretion of librarian. All pre-1801 hymnals cataloged and accessible through the website. Some hymns are manuscripts.

189. New York Public Library [1988]
Music Division
40 Lincoln Center Plaza, 3rd Floor
New York, New York 10023-7498
Ph: (212) 870-1650
Web: www.nypl.org/research/lpa/mus/mus.html

Institutional, Public
Size: 1,000

Details: Over 1,000 cataloged American and European hymnals.

190. Union Theological Seminary
Burke Library
3041 Broadway
New York, New York 10027
Contact: Head of Reference
Ph: (212) 280-1501
E-mail: refdesk@uts.columbia.edu
Web: www.uts.columbia.edu/burke_library
Catalog: See website

Institutional, Private
Size: 2,500
Date Range: 17th–20th
Lend: See details below
Copy: See details below

Details: The Sacred Music Collection includes the Hymn Society of America Collection. The Burke Library has several thousand hymnals, of which approximately 900 are in the Hymn Society of America Collection. The date range is seventeenth to twentieth centuries, with the majority of hymnals falling in the period of 1860 to 1985. The majority of hymnals are English-language with American imprints, but there is also a useful and interesting selection of non-English-language and/or non-U.S. imprints. The library collects new hymnals of all major U.S. denominations and some foreign hymnals. Hymnals cataloged from 1976 on are represented in SOPHIA, the online catalog of Union and General Theological Seminaries. Many of the pre-1976 catalog records are in the twenty-volume book catalog of the Union Theological Seminary, *Shelf List of the Union Theological Seminary Library . . . in Classification Order* and *Alphabetical Arrangement of Main Entries* (G. K. Hall, 1960). Papers of hymnologist Frederick Mayer Bird (1838–1908), five boxes. No finding aid.

Library does not lend to nonaffiliated visitors; interlibrary loan requests may be made by another library, but pre-1900 and all fragile hymnals do not circulate. Hymnals published from 1900 onwards may be copied if they are in good condition.

191. Nyack College
Bailey Library
1 South Blvd.
Nyack, New York 10960
Contact: Linda Poston, Director
Ph: (845) 358-1710
Fax: (845) 353-0817
E-mail: postonl@nyack.du

Institutional, Private
Size: 135
Date Range: 19th–20th
Lend: Yes
Copy: Yes

Web: www.nyackcollege.edu/library
Catalog: www.waldo.msus.edu

Details: The collection's hymnals represent various denominations and organizations.

192. Shaker Museum Foundation [1988]
Emma B. King Library
88 Shaker Museum Rd.
Old Chatham, New York 12136
Ph: (518) 794-9100
Fax: (518) 794-8621
Web: www.shakermuseumoldchat.org

Institutional, Private
Size: 250

Details: About 250 cataloged items. Strong emphasis on Shaker, many in letteral notation. Both printed and manuscript hymnals and some recordings of their songs.

Denominations: *Shaker*

193. American Baptist Historical Society
Colgate Historical Library
1106 S. Goodman St.
Rochester, New York 14620
Contact: Director
Ph: (716) 473-1740
Fax: (716) 473-1740 (phone ahead, please)
E-mail: abhs@crcds.edu
Web: www.crcds.edu/abhs

Institutional, Private
Size: 500
Date Range: 18th–20th
Lend: No
Copy: See details below

Details: About 500 volumes, over half words-only, many 1780–1860.

The collection emphasizes standard Protestant evangelical works, for example Watts, Rippon, *Sacred Harp*. Includes some Asian languages (Assamese, Burmese, Japanese, Sgaw Karen, Tamil).

The repository and library are open Monday–Friday 9 a.m.–5 p.m. Materials do not circulate. Items too fragile to copy must be read on site.

Denominations: *Baptist*

194. Colgate Rochester Crozer Divinity School
Ambrose Swasey Library
1100 S. Goodman St.
Rochester, New York 14620
Contact: Thomas Haverly, Associate Librarian for Public Services
Ph: (716) 271-1320
Fax: (716) 271-2166
E-mail: thaverly@crcds.edu
Web: www.crcds.edu

Institutional, Private
Size: 1,800
Date Range: 16th–20th
Lend: See details below
Copy: See details below

Details: Includes 190 German hymnals, sixteenth–twentieth centuries.

Materials lent/copied through interlibrary loan only to academic libraries and New York state public libraries. Rare or fragile materials do not circulate/copy.

Denominations: *Baptist, Catholic, Episcopal, Lutheran, Methodist*

195. Eastman School of Music
Sibley Music Library
University of Rochester
27 Gibbs St.
Rochester, New York 14604
Contact: David Peter Coppen, Special Collections Librarian
Ph: (585) 274-1335
Fax: (585) 274-1380
E-mail: copn@mail.rochester.edu
Web: www.rochester.edu/Eastman/sibley
Catalog: groucho.lib.rochester.edu

Institutional, Private
Size: 1,000
Date Range: 18th–20th
Lend: See details below
Copy: Yes

Details: Modern imprints represent all major denominations of Christian hymnody. Particularly strong in U.S. imprints of the late nineteenth century. About 300 are pre-1850.

Older items do not circulate, but copies or microform reproductions may be requested. Lending is subject to interlibrary lending regulations. Copying is subject to copyright law provisions.

196. University of Rochester
Rush Rhees Library
Dept. of Rare Books and Special Collections
Rochester, New York 14627
Contact: Director
Ph: (585) 275-4477
Fax: (585) 273-1032
E-mail: rarebks@rcl.lib.rochester.edu
Web: www.lib.rochester.edu/rbk/rarehome.htm
Catalog: See website

Institutional, Private
Size: 4
Date Range: 19th–early 20th
Lend: No
Copy: See details below

Details: William Channing Gannett Papers: Includes one box of manuscript material, four hymnals. Material relates to the publication of *Unity Hymns and Chorals,* W. C. Gannett, ed. (Chicago: 1880; rev. ed. 1911).

Will copy depending on condition of item.

Denominations: *Unitarian*

197. State University of New York at Stony Brook
Special Collections
Frank Melville, Jr. Memorial Library
Stony Brook, New York 11794
Contact: Kristen J. Nyitray, Head of Special Collections
Ph: (631) 632-7119
Fax: (631) 632-7116
E-mail: knyitray@notes.cc.sunysb.edu
Web: www.stonybrook.edu/library

Institutional, Public
Size: 200
Date Range: 19th–20th
Lend: See details below
Copy: See details below

Details: About 200 uncataloged hymnals and songbooks, nineteenth- and twentieth-century, mostly American.

Shelflist available. Open to visitors and researchers Monday–Friday by appointment. Will do some photocopying. Would consider exchange.

198. Syracuse University
Department of Special Collections
Bird Library, Room 600
222 Waverly Ave.
Syracuse, New York 13244-2010
Contact: Special Collections Librarian
Ph: (315) 443-2697
Fax: (315) 443-9510
E-mail: arents1@library.syr.edu
Web: libwww.syr.edu

Institutional, Private
Size: 27
Date Range: 19th–20th
Lend: No
Copy: See details below

Details: Although uncataloged, the Methodist hymnals represent a good example of the denomination's music during the nineteenth and twentieth centuries.

They may be used in Special Collections, and copied if physical condition and copyright status permit. Hymnals may also be loaned for exhibit purposes, but not research use unless the loan is to another department of special collections and the standing rules (no circulation, no photocopying) are applied.

Denominations: *Methodist Episcopal*

North Carolina

199. Appalachian State University
W. L. Eury Appalachian Collection
Belk Library
Boone, North Carolina 28608
Contact: Fred J. Hay, Appalachian Collection Librarian
Ph: (828) 262-4041

Institutional, Public
Size: 700
Date Range: 19th–20th
Lend: See details below
Copy: See details below

Fax: (828) 262-2553
E-mail: hayfj@appstate.edu
Web: www.library.appstate.edu/appcoll
Catalog: See website

Details: Collection is primarily shape-note. See the website for listing. Shape-note materials are noncirculating. Will photocopy limited amounts.

200. University of North Carolina [1988]
Institutional, Public
Size: 750
Date Range: 19th–20th
Music Library
106 Hill Hall, CB# 3320
Chapel Hill, North Carolina 27599
Contact: Music Librarian
Ph: (919) 966-1113
E-mail: music_reference@unc.edu
Web: www.lib.unc.edu/music

Details: The library has 250 partly cataloged hymnals, including the Annabel Morris Buchanan Collection of shape-note hymnals. Also 500 nineteenth- and twentieth-century tunebooks and gospel songbooks with emphasis on Southern and folk items 1816–.

201. Duke University
Institutional, Private
Size: 1,600
Date Range: 16th–21st
Lend: See details below
Copy: No
Divinity School Library
P.O. Box 90972
Durham, North Carolina 27708
Contact: Roger Loyd, Director
Ph: (919) 660-3450
Fax: (919) 681-7594
E-mail: roger.loyd@duke.edu
Web: www.lib.duke.edu/divinity
Catalog: www.lib.duke.edu/online_catalog.html

Details: The Baker Collection of Hymnology includes over 300 editions of Wesleyan and rare Wesley music books. A full description of the Baker Collection can be found in *Papers of the Hymn Society* 25 (1964): 26.

Most premodern hymnals are housed in Duke's Special Collections Library. Interlibrary loans will be approved on a case-by-case basis.

Denominations: *Anglican, Methodist*

202. Duke University — *Institutional, Private*
Rare Book, Manuscript, and Special Collections Library
Box 90185
Durham, North Carolina 27708
Size: 1,000
Date Range: 18th–20th
Lend: No
Copy: Yes
Contact: Research Services staff
Ph: (919) 660-5822
Fax: (919) 660-5934
E-mail: special-collection@duke.edu
Web: scriptorium.lib.duke.edu
Catalog: www.lib.duke.edu/online_catalog.html

Details: Mostly Methodist hymnals, some examples of Confederate hymnals. Closed-stacks (noncirculating) collection to be used in-house.

Denominations: *Methodist*

203. Lake Junaluska Conference and Retreat Center [1988] — *Institutional, Private*
Southeastern Jurisdiction of the United Methodist Church
P.O. Box 67
759 Lakeshore Dr.
Lake Junaluska, North Carolina 28745
Size: 500
Date Range: 1737–20th
Ph: (828) 452-2881 or (800) 222-4930
Fax: (828) 456-4040
E-mail: info@lakejunaluska.com
Web: www.lakejunaluska.com

Details: The center has 500 cataloged hymnals from 1737 from archives of predecessors of the United Methodist Church.

Denominations: *Methodist, United Methodist*

204. Presbyterian Historical Society
P.O. Box 849
Montreat, North Carolina 28757
Contact: Assistant Director for Reference/Technical Services
E-mail: refdesk@history.pcusa.org
Ph: (828) 669-7061
Fax: (828) 669-5369
Web: www.history.pcusa.org

Institutional, Private
Size: 100
Date Range: 1755–present
Lend: No
Copy: See details below

Details: The society has 100 hymnals and tunebooks, 1755–present, partly cataloged. Will copy less than fifty pages.

Denominations: *Presbyterian Church in the United States, Presbyterian Church (U.S.A.)*

205. Leonard A. Smith
5700 Tully Ct.
Raleigh, North Carolina 27609
Ph: (919) 848-9493
E-mail: CarLeoSmith@aol.com

Individual
Size: 545
Date Range: 19th–20th
Lend: No
Copy: Yes

Details: The Cecil E. Lapo Collection includes all full editions of *Hymns Ancient and Modern* (except 1875) and other British hymnals. Fourteen singing school oblongs. Many nineteenth-century Methodist hymnals. Books of worship and liturgies. Many hymnology books. A 1684 Sternhold and Hopkins.

Denominations: *Anglican, Methodist*

206. Wingate University
E. K. Smith Library
P.O. Box 219
Wingate, North Carolina 28174
Contact: Jimm Wetherbee, Information Systems Librarian
Ph: (704) 233-8097
E-mail: jimm@wingate.edu
Web: library.wingate.edu
Catalog: eksplorer.wingate.edu

Institutional, Private
Size: 60
Date Range: 1816–1980
Lend: Yes
Copy: Yes

Details: Almost all English-language and American Protestant hymnals. Of these, most are hymnals that are or at one time would have been used by Baptist congregations in the Wingate area, although hymnals from Presbyterians, Methodists, Episcopalians, and other mainline denominations are also represented.

Denominations: *Baptist, Episcopal, Methodist, Presbyterian*

207. Moravian Music Foundation
Peter Memorial Library
457 S. Church St.
P.O. Box L, Salem Station
Winston-Salem, North Carolina 27108
Contact: Nola Reed Knouse, Director
Ph: (336) 725-0651
Fax: (336) 725-4514
E-mail: nknouse@mcsp.org
Web: www.moravianmusic.org

Institutional, Private
Size: 2,000
Date Range: 16th–20th
Lend: No
Copy: No

Details: The library has 2,000 hymnals, all cataloged in the system, including hymnals from the Moravian Church in various countries. Irving Lowens Collection of about 1,000 early American tunebooks and 10,000 manuscripts and early imprints of music used/composed by Moravians in America and Europe, especially in the eighteenth and early nineteenth centuries.

Library is open to researchers Monday–Friday 9 a.m.–noon, 1:30–4:30 p.m. Please make appointment.

Denominations: *Moravian*

Ohio

208. Baldwin-Wallace College
Jones Music Library
275 Eastland Rd.
Berea, Ohio 44017
Contact: Director
Ph: (440) 826-2375
Fax: (440) 826-6250

Institutional, Private
Size: 75
Date Range: 19th–20th
Lend: See details below
Copy: No

E-mail: jonesml@bw.edu
Web: www.bw.edu/academics/libraries/jones

Details: Approximately seventy-five volumes of hymnals of various denominations, almost all twentieth-century. The United Methodist Historical Collection once housed in the library has been transferred to the East Ohio Conference United Methodist Archives Center (www.owu.edu/~librweb/spserve.htm).

Materials circulate only to students and staff. Will lend if materials are not fragile.

209. Cincinnati Bible College & Seminary
G. M. Elliott Library
2700 Glenway Ave.
Cincinnati, Ohio 45204
Contact: James Lloyd, Director
Ph: (513) 244-8180
Fax: (513) 244-8434
E-mail: jim.lloyd@cincybible.edu
Web: www.cincybible.edu/cbclibrary

Institutional, Private
Size: 1,064
Date Range: 1786–present
Lend: See details below
Copy: See details below

Details: The collection consists mainly of nineteenth- and twentieth-century Protestant hymnals, tunebooks, psalters, etc., both with and without music. Emphasis on Restoration Movement (Stone-Campbell Movement).

Willing to copy and lend materials depending on condition of item.

Denominations: *Christian Church (Disciples of Christ), Christian Churches and Churches of Christ, Churches of Christ*

210. Cincinnati Museum Center
Historical Society Library
1301 Western Ave.
Cincinnati, Ohio 45203
Contact: Curator of Printed Works
Ph: (513) 287-7098

Institutional, Private
Size: 130
Date Range: 19th–early 20th
Lend: No
Copy: See details below

Fax: (513) 297-7095
E-mail: library@cincymuseum.org
Web: www.cincymuseum.org/research

Details: Most of the hymnals are in English or German, though there is one in Ojibwa and Delaware.

Access to the sixty uncataloged hymnals of the Nippert Collection (German Methodism) is by appointment only. The rest of the collection is open to the public Monday–Friday noon–5 p.m., Saturday 10 a.m.–5 p.m.

Denominations: *German Methodist*

211. The Jacob Rader Marcus Center of the American Jewish Archives
3101 Clifton Ave.
Cincinnati, Ohio 45220
Contact: Kevin Proffitt, Chief Archivist
Ph: (513) 221-1875
Fax: (513) 221-7812
E-mail: kproffitt@cn.huc.edu
Web: www.americanjewisharchives.org

Institutional, Private
Date Range: 18th–20th
Lend: Yes
Copy: Yes

Details: The archival and manuscript holdings of the Marcus Center include over 675 major manuscript collections and nearly 15,000 smaller collections. The Archives holds nearly 3,000 audio and video recordings consisting of oral histories, lectures, religious services, and music. The collection includes the papers of Louis Wolsey, chairman of the Central Conference of American Rabbis' Committee on the *Union Hymnal* when the hymnal was revised in 1946.

Denominations: *Judaic*

212. Case Western Reserve University
Kulas Music Library
11118 Bellflower Rd.

Institutional, Private
Size: 50
Date Range: 16th–20th
Lend: Yes

Cleveland, Ohio 44106-7106
Contact: Stephen Toombs, Information Manager
Ph: (216) 368-2403
E-mail: sht@po.cwru.edu
Web: www.cwru.edu/UL/Subjects/MUSC/musc.htm
Catalog: catalog.cwru.edu

Copy: No

Details: The library has a printed bibliography of early items.

213. Cleveland Public Library
Special Collections and Fine Arts Departments
325 Superior Ave.
Cleveland, Ohio 44114
Contact: Special Collections/ Fine Arts Librarian
Ph: (216) 623-2848 or (216) 623-2818
Fax: (216) 623-2976
E-mail: Special.Collections@cpl.org
Web: www.cpl.org

Institutional, Public
Size: 2,000
Date Range: 16th–21st
Lend: No
Copy: See details below

Details: 28-drawer index of hymns, 3-drawer index of Christmas carols; both are noncirculating. Charge for copying.

214. Western Reserve Historical Society
Archives Library
10825 E. Boulevard
Cleveland, Ohio 44106
Contact: Reference Division
Ph: (216) 721-5722
Fax: (216) 721-5702
E-mail: reference@wrhs.org
Web: www.wrhs.org/sites/library.htm

Institutional, Private
Size: 500
Date Range: 19th
Lend: No
Copy: Yes

Details: Nineteenth-century hymnals including general, English, German, Japanese, Native American, and 438 Shaker hymnals.

***Denominations:** Shaker*

215. Ohio Historical Society
Archives/Library Division
1982 Velma Ave.
Columbus, Ohio 43211-2497
Contact: Research Services
Ph: (614) 297-2510
Fax: (614) 297-2546
E-mail: ohsref@ohiohistory.org
Web: www.ohiohistory.org

Institutional, Private
Size: 383
Date Range: 19th–20th
Lend: No
Copy: Yes

Details: The society has 383 nineteenth- and twentieth-century hymnals. Special collections include 10 hymnals printed in German from the Society of Separatists of Zoar and 9 Shaker hymnals. The New Jerusalem Church is also represented.

No lending of the collections, but will photocopy pages at 25¢ per page to a limit of 25 pages.

Denominations: *Baptist, Christian Church (Disciples of Christ), Christian Science, Lutheran, Mennonite, Methodist, New Church, Reformed Church in the United States, Shaker, Society of Separatists of Zoar*

216. Trinity Lutheran Seminary
Hamma Library
2199 E. Main St.
Columbus, Ohio 43209-2334
Contact: Senior Librarian
Ph: (614) 235-4136
Fax: (614) 238-0263
E-mail: TLSLibrary@trinity.capital.edu
Web: www.trinity.capital.edu
Catalog: www.tcgc.capital.edu

Institutional, Private
Size: See details below
Date Range: 18th–present
Lend: See details below
Copy: See details below

Details: Many of the hymnals were acquired to support the divinity degree, but the majority were given to the library by pastors, scholars, and friends of the seminary. Since the historical background of the seminary is German Lutheran, hymnals used in the German-speaking countries during this same era were added intentionally by the then-current librarians and professors or in later archival endeavors. The collection fills five to six sections of shelving, approximately thirty-five shelves. The American Lutheran strains are particularly well represented, especially those hymnals published in the German and English languages. The collection is comprehensive relating to titles published by or used in Lutheran churches in Ohio and adjacent states. Hamma Library continues to acquire new hymnals from the various North American denominational traditions. It gladly accepts gifts that complement or fill in gaps in the existing collection and occasionally orders items. Since many of the hymnals belong to liturgical church traditions, Hamma Library has attempted to collect the liturgical service or altar books which complement the specific hymnals but which were separately published.

The cataloged records, one-fourth to one-third of the collection, can be accessed through the Internet by searching the Voyager online public access catalog of the Theological Consortium of Greater Columbus. There are no finding aids for the uncataloged titles. The hymnals in the online catalog which are housed in the TLS Main Collection (stacks) are available through OCLC interlibrary loan or conventional interlibrary loan for a period of one month. Other collection locations require in-library use.

Denominations: *Lutheran*

217. United Theological Seminary
Memorial Library
1810 Harvard Blvd.
Dayton, Ohio 45406-4599
Contact: Director
Ph: (937) 278-5817
Fax: (937) 275-5701
E-mail: library@united.edu
Web: library.united.edu/library.asp

Institutional, Public
Size: 800
Date Range: 19th–20th
Lend: See details below
Copy: See details below

Details: About 800 volumes cataloged. Major strengths are hymnals and songbooks of the predecessors to the United Methodist Church, nineteenth century through 1968. Early hymnals are words-only, both English and German editions. Miscellaneous other denominational hymnals and revival songbooks, some in the E. S. Lorenz Collection.

Newer hymnals sent on interlibrary loan forms. Will photocopy at cost at discretion of librarian. Open to visitors and researchers Monday–Friday 8:30 a.m.–4:30 p.m.

Denominations: *Methodist, United Methodist*

218. University of Dayton
The Marian Library
300 College Park
Dayton, Ohio 45469-1390
Contact: Thomas A. Thompson
Ph: (937) 229-4252
Fax: (937) 229-4258
E-mail: Thomas.Thompson@udayton.edu
Web: www.udayton.edu/mary
Catalog: library.udayton.edu

Institutional, Private
Size: 200
Date Range: 19th–20th
Lend: See details below
Copy: See details below

Details: Catholic devotional materials in English, French, German, and Spanish. The library does not lend rare or fragile materials. In most cases, copies will be made.

Denominations: *Catholic*

219. Methodist Theological School in Ohio
John W. Dickhart Library
3801 Columbus Pike
Delaware, Ohio 43015
Contact: Paul Schrodt, Director
Ph: (740) 363-1146
E-mail: pschrodt@mtso.edu
Web: www.mtso.edu/library/library.asp
Catalog: See website

Institutional, Private
Size: 142
Date Range: 19th–20th
Lend: No
Copy: See details below

Details: The collection, dating from ca. 1800 to 1964, represents the United Methodist Church and its antecedents.

Will copy a few pages and damage to books will not result.

Denominations: *United Methodist*

220. Rutherford B. Hayes Presidential Center
Spiegel Grove
Fremont, Ohio 43420-2796
Contact: Head Librarian
Ph: (419) 332-2801
Fax: (410) 332-4952
E-mail: hayeslib@rbhayes.org
Web: www.rbhayes.org
Catalog: maurice.bgsu.edu

Institutional, Private
Size: 140
Date Range: 19th
Lend: No
Copy: Yes

Details: Mostly English, a few German. Nearly all Protestant, with Presbyterian and Methodist Episcopal well represented (eight to ten titles each). About twenty-five are specifically for Sunday school. Four are designated as soldiers' songbooks and hymnals. Eighty percent are from the nineteenth century.

Denominations: *Methodist Episcopal, Presbyterian*

221. James T. Burson
4898 Harrisburg
Grove City, Ohio 43123
Ph: (614) 871-0277
Fax: (614) 445-3767
E-mail: bursonj@fcesc.org

Individual
Size: 3,200
Date Range: early 18th–20th
Lend: Yes
Copy: Yes

Details: Many duplicates, willing to trade. Oblong tunebooks are of special interest; 257 tunebook titles in this collection.

222. Terry E. Miller
2005 Willow Ridge Circle
Kent, Ohio 44240
Ph: (330) 673-3763
Fax: (330) 673-4434
E-mail: tmiller1@kent.edu

Individual
Size: 300
Date Range: 19th–20th
Lend: No
Copy: See details below

Details: About 300 songsters of singing school tradition (50 words-only), emphasis on shape-note and numeric notation, 1815–1985. Also about 60 hymnals (no round notation). Open to researchers by appointment. Will consider exchange.

223. Oberlin College
Dictionary of American
Hymnology Project
Oberlin College Library
Oberlin, Ohio 44074
Contact: Mary Louise VanDyke
Ph: (440) 775-8622
Fax: (440) 775-6586
E-mail: dhymns@oberlin.edu
Web: www.oberlin.edu/library/libncollect/DAH.html

Institutional, Private
Size: 1,200
Date Range: 19th–20th
Lend: No
Copy: See details below

Details: Hymnals from Oberlin College, the Hymn Society, and the Dictionary of American Hymnology Project (DAH) are all in this collection. Among the holdings are hymnal companions, studies, booklets, and facsimilies. Recordings, vocal arrangements, and many dissertations on microfilm are also available. Hymnal languages include Armenian, Burmese, Czech, Dakota, French, German, Gilbertese, Italian, Japanese, Latin, Ojibwa, Thai, and Welsh. Strengths are temperance, abolition, children's, and mission hymnals of the nineteenth century. Will photocopy on librarian's approval.

The DAH provides data related to hymns and hymn writers as well as the history of congregational song in America. The project comprises four sources for research: an index of first lines of hymns from 1640 to 1978 with a supplementary index 1978 to present; a bibliography of some 5,000 hymnals published in America (1,817 denominational and 3,192 nondenominational); an author file; and a biographical file. Hymnals of many languages have been indexed; the DAH is not limited to only those hymnals printed in English. The DAH is expected to be available on CD-ROM.

224. Daniel Jay Grimminger
P.O. Box 1
Paris, Ohio 44669
Ph: (330) 862-2064
E-mail: grimminger@aol.com

Individual
Size: 400
Date Range: 18th–20th
Lend: No
Copy: Yes

Details: Lutheran holdings are mainly those of the early American German immigrants. Some editions of the Christopher Saur

Marburger Gesangbuch and the *Muhlenburg Erbauliche Lieder Sammlung* are earliest volumes held. Outside this interest area, the collection contains hymnals of other denominations, mainly those with a strong emphasis on the German chorale. In addition to the 400 hymnals, the collection also includes a much wider collection of books, journals, and music scores relating to hymnody, liturgy, theology, and Johann Sebastian Bach. Interested in trading and buying.

Denominations: *Lutheran, Moravian*

225. Allen Viehmeyer
1856 Alverne Dr.
Poland, Ohio 44514-1405
E-mail: laviehme@cc.ysu.edu

Individual
Size: 100
Date Range: 18th–early 20th
Lend: See details below
Copy: See details below

Details: This collection consists of hymnals and music books in the German language, or bilingual German/English, printed in North America between 1730 and 1920. It includes German Baptist and German Catholic hymnals. These are all North American imprints; there are very few European hymnals. The only English-language hymnals are Amish, Mennonite, and Hutterite; they were all published after 1920. Of special interest is Ephrata hymnology, and books and hymnals (some as microfilm or photocopy) dealing with pietistic hymns.

Willing to lend materials that are not too fragile for shipping; willing to copy materials that are not too fragile for copying.

Denominations: *Amish, Brethren, Catholic, German Baptist, German Seventh Day Baptist, Hutterite, Lutheran, Mennonite, Moravian, Reformed, Society of Separatists of Zoar*

226. Shaker Historical Society/ Museum
Nord Memorial Library
16740 S. Park Blvd.
Shaker Heights, Ohio 44120
Contact: Librarian
Ph: (216) 921-1201

Institutional, Private
Size: 50
Date Range: 19th–20th
Lend: See details below
Copy: See details below

Fax: (216) 921-2615
E-mail: shakhist@bright.net
Web: www.cwru.edu/affil/shakhist/shaker.htm

Details: *The Village Harmony, or New-England Repository of Sacred Musick* ("Created by Lewis Edwards, Book-binder, 10 Rods North West of the State House, Hartford"). Signed by James Prescott, who brought it from Connecticut to the North Union Shaker Community (founded 1822).

Bennett, Rufus, and Lisette Walker, eds., *Funeral Hymns of the North Union Shakers—Record of Deaths from 1827–1899* (handwritten manuscript).

The library lends to members or students who deposit $20 (returned when materials are returned). Copying is 25¢ per page for nonmembers; the library is reluctant to make copies of rare books.

Denominations: *Shaker*

227. St. Luke Lutheran Mission
539 W. North St.
Springfield, Ohio 45504
Contact: Louis Voigt
Ph: (937) 399-9969

Institutional, Private
Size: 1,047
Date Range: 17th–20th
Lend: Yes
Copy: Yes

Details: The collection contains 1,047 uncataloged hymnals classed by German city of origin, plus 175 volumes on German hymnology. Special strengths in German dictionaries and Lutheran hymnal bibliography. Will photocopy and mail suitable books. Visitors welcome.

Denominations: *Lutheran*

228. Wittenberg University
Thomas Library
Ward St. at N. Wittenberg Ave.
P.O. Box 7207
Springfield, Ohio 45501-7207
Contact: Norman Pearson,
Head of Technical Services

Institutional, Private
Size: 1,085
Date Range: 1523–1972
Lend: No
Copy: Yes

Ph: (937) 327-7529
E-mail: npearson@mail.wittenberg.edu
Web: www6.wittenberg.edu/lib

Details: German liturgies and psalters, Kirchenordnungen, mission and diaspora hymnals, child and youth hymnals. Hymnals of sixteenth–twentieth-century Germany.

American Lutheran liturgies and hymnals (English and German language); many Lutheran denominations; non-Lutheran English hymnals, psalms, and tunebooks. Hymnals and liturgies in other languages (primarily Danish, Finnish, Norwegian, and Swedish). Hymnals of later date ranges will be added to the collection. Uncataloged. See Voigt, Louis, *Hymnals at Wittenberg* (Springfield: Chantry Music Press, 1975).

Hymnals are a part of Special Collections. Copying is 10¢ per page, plus $5 service charge. Open Monday–Friday 9 a.m.–3 p.m.

Denominations: *Augustana Synod, Danish Synods, Evangelical Lutheran Ministerium of New York, Evangelical Lutheran Ministerium of Pennsylvania, Evangelical Lutheran Synods (Iowa, Missouri, Ohio, Tennessee, Wisconsin); General Council of the Evangelical Lutheran Church in North America, General Synod of the Evangelical Lutheran Church in the USA, Lutheran Church in America, Lutheran Synod of Buffalo, Norwegian Synods, United Lutheran Church, United Synod of the Evangelical Lutheran Church in the South*

229. Louis Bertoni
P.O. Box 298
Vermilion, Ohio 44089
Ph: (440) 967-5066
E-mail: lebertoni@aol.com

Individual
Size: 1,350
Date Range: late 18th–20th
Lend: Yes
Copy: Yes

Details: Partly cataloged American hymnals. Will mail and send on interlibrary loan form. Will photocopy. The collection is now housed in Zoar, Ohio, and can be used by appointment.

Denominations: *Lutheran*

230. Otterbein College
Courtright Memorial Library
138 W. Main St.
Westerville, Ohio 43081
Contact: Doris Ebbert, Collection Development Librarian (Liaison for Music Department)
Ph: (614) 823-1314
Fax: (614) 823-1921
E-mail: debbert@otterbein.edu
Web: www.otterbein.edu/resources/library/library.htm

Institutional, Private
Size: 68
Date Range: late 19th–20th
Lend: See details below
Copy: No

Details: Thirty-four circulating and thirty-four in the archives, which do not circulate.

Denominations: *United Brethren in Christ, United Methodist*

Oklahoma

231. Oklahoma Baptist University
Mabee Learning Center
500 W. University St.
Shawnee, Oklahoma 74804
Contact: Tom Terry, Archivist
Ph: (405) 878-2254
Fax: (405) 878-2270
E-mail: tom_terry@mail.okbu.edu
Web: www.okbu.edu/library
Catalog: See website

Institutional, Private
Size: 200
Date Range: 1850–1940
Lend: No
Copy: See details below

Details: B. B. McKinney Collection: Baptist hymnals and tunebooks, ca.1850–1940; also hymns by McKinney.

Use of collection must be under supervision of the Archives staff. Only noncopyrighted materials may be copied. Cost will be determined at time of request.

Denominations: *Baptist*

232. Oral Roberts University
John D. Messick Learning Resources Center

Institutional, Private
Size: 2,000
Date Range: 18th–19th

7777 S. Lewis Ave.
Tulsa, Oklahoma 74171
Contact: William W. Jernigan,
Dean of Learning Resources
Ph: (918) 495-6723
Fax: (918) 495-6893
E-mail: wjernigan@oru.edu
Web: www.oru.edu/university/library
Catalog: See website

Lend: Yes
Copy: Yes

Details: Strong in Pentecostal and charismatic items.

Denominations: *Pentecostal*

233. Phillips Theological Seminary [1988]
Library
901 North Mingo Rd.
Tulsa, Oklahoma 74116-5612
Ph: (918) 631-3905
E-mail: ptslibrary@ptstulsa.edu
Web: www.ptstulsa.edu

Institutional, Private
Size: 400

Details: About 400 cataloged hymnals of many denominations. Emphasis on gospel music, 1920s–1940s.

Ontario

234. Jim Willis
94 Lillian Crescent
Barrie, Ontario L4N 5H7
Canada
E-mail: jwillis@drlogick.com

Individual
Size: 20
Date Range: 20th
Lend: No
Copy: Yes

Details: Highlights include:
Melodies of Praise (Springfield, Mass.: Gospel Publishing House, 1957);
Tabernacle Hymns No. 4 (Chicago, Ill.: Tabernacle Publishing Company, 1944);
Alexander's Hymns No. 3 (New York: Fleming H. Revell Co., 1915?);

The Hymn Book with Music (n.p.: The Anglican Church of Canada, 1938);
Hymns of the Living Faith: Hymnal of the Free Methodist Church (Winona Lake, Ind.: Light & Life Press, 1951);
Crowning Glory Hymnal (Grand Rapids, Mich.: Singspiration Music/Zondervan, 1965);
Service Book and Hymnal (Minneapolis: Augsburg Publishing House, 1958);
The Book of Praise (Don Mills, Ontario: Presbyterian Church of Canada, 1972);
The Hymnal for Worship and Celebration (Irving, Tex.: Word Music, 1989);
Hymnal: A Worship Book (Scottdale, Pa.: Mennonite Publishing House, 1992);
The Lutheran Hymnal (St. Louis: Concordia Publishing House, 1941);
Church Hymnal Mennonite (Scottdale, Pa.: Mennonite Publishing House, 1927);
The Mennonite Hymnal (Scottdale, Pa.: Herald Press, 1969);
The Song Book of the Salvation Army (London: Salvationist Publishing and Supplies Ltd., 1955).

Denominations: *Anglican, Mennonite, Presbyterian, Salvation Army*

235. Canadian National Institute for the Blind
Music Library
1929 Bayview Ave.
Toronto, Ontario M6S 3T6
Canada
Contact: Music Librarian
Ph: (416) 480-7631
Fax: (416) 480-7700
E-mail: library@lib.cnib.ca
Web: www.cnib.ca/library
Catalog: See website

Institutional, Private
Size: 50
Date Range: 19th–20th
Lend: Yes
Copy: See details below

Details: Braille hymnals, some with Braille music.

Not all of the holdings are in the Web catalog. Available for interlibrary loan. Most materials produced by the CNIB are available for sale.

Denominations: *Anglican, Lutheran, United Church of Canada*

236. Toronto Public Library
Toronto Reference Library
789 Yonge St.
Toronto, Ontario M4W 2G8
Canada
Contact: Reference Desk
Ph: (416) 393-7131
E-mail: See website
Web: www.tpl.toronto.on.ca

Institutional, Public
Size: 400
Date Range: 19th–20th
Lend: No
Copy: No

Details: Emphasis on Canadian hymnals, but includes American and British publications. Includes hymnals in languages of indigenous peoples.

237. Victoria University in the University of Toronto
Emmanuel College Library
75 Queen's Park Crescent E.
Toronto, Ontario M5S 1K7
Canada
Contact: Karen Wishart, Librarian
Ph: (416) 585-4551
Fax: (416) 585-4516
E-mail: karen.wishart@utoronto.ca
Web: library.vicu.utoronto.ca/emmanuel

Institutional, Public
Size: 1,700
Date Range: 18th–20th
Lend: See details below
Copy: See details below

Details: Primarily North American and British hymnals, songbooks, and psalters. Hymnology materials are not kept as a separate collection. Collection strengths are in early Methodist books, temperance materials, and publications of the United Church of Canada.

Books published by the Wesley brothers during their lifetimes are included in a separate Wesleyana collection, founded upon the personal collection of the Rev. Richard Green (1829–1907). The personal collection of Dr. Stanley Osborne has recently been added to the library.

Please use interlibrary loan requests for items in the circulating collection. Requests for photocopies of pages from rare books may be granted if the book can be copied safely.

Denominations: *Methodist, Presbyterian, United Church of Canada*

Pennsylvania

238. The Moravian Archives
41 W. Locust St.
Bethlehem, Pennsylvania 18018
Contact: Archivist
Ph: (610) 866-3255
Fax: (610) 866-9210
Web: www.moravianchurcharchives.com

Institutional, Private
Size: 1,000
Date Range: 16th–20th
Lend: No
Copy: See details below

Details: Some of the hymnals come from mission areas and are in non-European languages.

Will not copy from bound volumes.

Denominations: *Moravian*

239. Moravian College and Theological Seminary
Reeves Library
1200 Main St.
Bethlehem, Pennsylvania 18018
Contact: Director
Ph: (610) 861-1541
Fax: (610) 861-1577
Web: home.moravian.edu/public/reeves

Institutional, Private
Size: 400
Date Range: 16th–20th
Lend: See details below
Copy: See details below

Details: Groenfeldt Moravian Collection: 400 volumes on Moravian hymnody and Moravian music in various languages. Circulating materials are available on interlibrary loan.

Denominations: *Moravian*

240. D. DeWitt Wasson
110 Laurel Place
Cornwall, Pennsylvania 17016
Ph: (717) 272-0685
E-mail: ddwas@mbcomp.com

Individual
Size: 468
Date Range: 19th–20th
Lend: No
Copy: No

Details: All hymnals are cataloged and included in D. DeWitt Wasson, *Hymntune Index and Related Hymn Materials* (Lanham, Md.: Scarecrow Press, 1998).

241. Elizabethtown College
High Library
One Alpha Dr.
Elizabethtown, Pennsylvania 17022
Contact: Reference Librarian/Archivist
Ph: (717) 361-1453
E-mail: ask-a-librarian@etown.edu
Web: www.etown.edu/library

Institutional, Private
Size: 125
Date Range: 1752–present
Lend: No
Copy: Yes

Details: The library has 125 cataloged psalters and hymnals in German and English. 75 percent in German without music. Earliest imprint is 1752.

Open to visitors and researchers Monday–Friday 8:30 a.m.–5 p.m. Rare books do not circulate.

Denominations: *Church of the Brethren*

242. Lutheran Theological Seminary
A. R. Wentz Library
66 Seminary Ridge
Gettysburg, Pennsylvania 17325
Contact: Bonnie L. VanDelinder, Librarian
Ph: (717) 338-3018
Fax: (717) 337-1611
E-mail: bvandelinder@ltsg.edu
Web: www.ltsg.edu/sem

Institutional, Private
Size: 250
Date Range: 18th–20th
Lend: See details below
Copy: See details below

Details: Pre-1940 Lutheran hymnals and liturgy books published in the United States; about half are words-only. Many nineteenth- and early-twentieth-century items.

Will lend circulating materials, but not those in special collections. Will make photocopies at 10¢ per page.

Denominations: *Lutheran*

243. Mennonite Historians of Eastern Pennsylvania [1988]
Institutional, Private
Date Range: 18th–20th
565 Yoder Rd.
P.O. Box 82
Harleysville, Pennsylvania 19438-0082
Ph: (215) 256-3020
Fax: (215) 256-3023
E-mail: info@mhep.org
Web: www.mhep.org

Details: Mennonite and Amish hymnals and singing books, 1751–. Several American editions of Amish *Ausbund* (1751, 1767, 1785, 1815, 1834, 1846, and later). Manuscript singing books, with fraktur letters and illuminations, include original compositions from late eighteenth–early nineteenth centuries. Two *Zionitischer Weyrauchs-Hügel* (1739), and all editions of the *Zion Harfe* (1803, 1811, 1821, 1834, 1848, 1870, 1904). Also have the Franconia Conference Mennonite hymnal.

Denominations: *Amish, Mennonite*

244. State Library of Pennsylvania
Rare Book Collection
Forum Bldg. P.O. Box 1601
Harrisburg, Pennsylvania 17105
Contact: Reference Librarian
Ph: (717) 783-5982
Fax: (717) 783-2070
E-mail: ra-reference@state.pa.us
Web: www.statelibrary.state.pa.us

Institutional, Public
Size: 200
Date Range: 1740–1840
Lend: No
Copy: Yes

Details: About 200 uncataloged volumes, including a major emphasis on early Pennsylvania imprints to 1850, three Ephrata manuscript music books (two from Ephrata, 1740, and one from Snow Hill, 1840). Some shape-note, some words-only. Some British and German hymnals.

Open to researchers by appointment only. Will photocopy.

***Denominations:** German Seventh Day Baptist, Lutheran, Moravian, Reformed, Schwenkfelder, Seventh Day Baptist*

245. Juniata College
Beeghly Library
1700 Moore St.
Huntingdon, Pennsylvania 16652
Contact: Hedda Durnbaugh, College Archivist
Ph: (814) 641-3484
Fax: (814) 641-3435
E-mail: library@juniata.edu
Web: www.juniata.edu/pages/library

Institutional, Private
Size: 200
Date Range: 17th–20th
Lend: No
Copy: See details below

Details: Multiple editions (mostly German), including ten editions of *Ausbund* and other German hymnals. Also includes nineteenth-century tunebooks.

Copying only if physical condition of item permits.

***Denominations:** Church of the Brethren, German Reformed, German Seventh Day Baptist, Lutheran, Mennonite*

246. Hedda Durnbaugh
P.O. Box 484
James Creek, Pennsylvania 16657
Ph: (814) 658-3222
Fax: (814) 658-3222
E-mail: durnbaughh@juniata.edu

Individual
Size: 200
Date Range: 17th–20th
Lend: No
Copy: See details below

Details: Danish, Dutch, Finnish, German, Norwegian, Swedish, polyglot hymnals.

Copying only if possible without damage to item.

Denominations: *Church of the Brethren, German Reformed, Lutheran, Mennonite*

247. Franklin & Marshall College
Shadek-Fackenthal Library
P.O. Box 3003
Lancaster, Pennsylvania 17604
Contact: Ann W. Upton, College Archivist and Special Collections Librarian
Ph: (717) 291-4225
Fax: (717) 291-4160
E-mail: a_upton@fandm.edu
Web: library.fandm.edu
Catalog: See website

Institutional, Private
Size: 120
Date Range: 1747–1900
Lend: No
Copy: See details below

Details: The German American Imprint Collection includes 120 German hymnals published in Pennsylvania which date from 1747 to 1900. It is largely uncataloged.

Photocopies can be made if the originals are not fragile. Please contact the librarian to learn if the library has a hymnal for which you are searching.

Denominations: *German Reformed*

248. Lancaster Mennonite Historical Society
2215 Millstream Rd.
Lancaster, Pennsylvania 17602
Contact: Librarian
Ph: (717) 393-9745
Fax: (717) 393-8751
E-mail: lmhs@lmhs.org
Web: www.lmhs.org

Institutional, Private
Size: 4,500
Date Range: 18th–20th
Lend: No
Copy: Yes

Details: Martin E. Ressler Collection: A large collection of Amish, Mennonite, Church of the Brethren, and Brethren in Christ hymnals. Also many commercially produced books of nineteenth- and twentieth-century gospel songs and Sunday school songs. About 1,100 hymnological works in the main part of the library.

Photocopy charge: 25¢ per copy and $5 handling fee plus postage. Will bill.

Open Tuesday–Saturday 8:30 a.m.–4:30 p.m.

Denominations: *Amish, Church of the Brethren, Brethren in Christ, Mennonite*

249. Lancaster Theological Seminary
Evangelical and Reformed
Historical Society
555 W. James St.
Lancaster, Pennsylvania 17603
Contact: Archivist
Ph: (717) 290-8704
Fax: (717) 393-4254
E-mail: erhs@lts.org
Web: www.erhs.info
Catalog: www.lts.org/Library/library.html

Institutional, Private
Size: 400
Date Range: 17th–20th
Lend: See details below
Copy: See details below

Details: Highlights include: Philip Schaff's annotated copy of his *Deutsches Gesangbuch* (Philadelphia: Lindsay und Klakiston; Berlin: Wiegandt & Grieben, 1859); Lewis H. Steiner's manuscript copy of his *Cantate Domino* (Boston: O. Ditson, 1859); manuscript English translation of Philip Schaff's *Deutsches Gesangbuch;* Pennsylvania German imprints of Saur, Billmeyer, etc.; copy of *Marburger Gesangbuch* (Marburg und Frankfurt: H. L. Brönner, 1770) bound in vellum, stamped with a heart and flowers and hand-colored.

Materials in circulating collection can be borrowed. Materials in good condition can be photocopied.

Denominations: *Evangelical and Reformed, German Reformed, Netherlands Reformed, Reformed Church in Germany, Reformed Church in the United States*

250. Philadelphia Biblical University
Masland Learning Resource Center
200 Manor Ave.
Langhorne, Pennsylvania 19047
Contact: Dorothy M. Black, Public Services Librarian
Ph: (215) 702-4375
Fax: (215) 702-4374
E-mail: Library@pbu.edu
Web: www.library.pbu.edu

Institutional, Private
Size: 1,057
Date Range: 18th–19th
Lend: Yes

Details: Over 1,000 eighteenth- and nineteenth-century American hymnals. All hymnals circulate.

251. Lititz Moravian Church
8 Church Square
Lititz, Pennsylvania 17543
Ph: (717) 626-8515
E-mail: litmorav@desupernet.net
Web: www.moravian.org/find_us/congregations.html

Institutional, Private
Size: 100
Date Range: 18th–20th
Lend: Yes
Copy: Yes

Details: Some hymnals printed in English and some in German, dating from the early eighteenth century through the twentieth century.

***Denominations:** Moravian*

252. Schwenkfelder Library & Heritage Center
Schwenkfelder Library
105 Seminary St.
Pennsburg, Pennsylvania 18073
Contact: Archivist
Ph: (215) 679-3103
Fax: (215) 679-8175
E-mail: info@schwenkfelder.com
Web: www.schwenkfelder.com

Institutional, Private
Size: 150
Date Range: 17th–20th
Lend: See details below
Copy: See details below

Details: Manuscript and print version of *Neu-Eingerichtetes Gesangbuch* (n.p.: Christopher Saur, 1762). Also manuscript hymnals with fraktur bookplates.

Materials lent and/or photocopied based on condition of original.

Denominations: *Lutheran, Mennonite, Moravian, Reformed, Schwenkfelder*

253. **Free Library of Philadelphia [1988]**
Music Dept.
1901 Vine St.
Philadelphia, Pennsylvania 19103
Ph: (215) 686-5322
Web: www.library.phila.gov

Institutional, Public
Size: 1,000
Date Range: 18th–20th

Details: The library has 1,000 hymnals, tunebooks, and songbooks, including works by William Billings, Andrew Law, Isaiah Thomas, and John Wyeth.

254. **German Society of Pennsylvania**
Joseph Horner Memorial Library
611 Spring Garden St.
Philadelphia, Pennsylvania 19123
Contact: Laurie Wolfe
Ph: (215) 627-2332
E-mail: contact@germansociety.org
Web: www.germansociety.org/library.html

Institutional, Private
Size: 120
Date Range: 19th–20th
Lend: No
Copy: Yes

255. **Historical Society of Pennsylvania**
1300 Locust St.
Philadelphia, Pennsylvania 19107
Contact: Rachel Onuf, Director of Archives
Ph: (215) 732-6200
Fax: (215) 732-2680
E-mail: ronuf@hsp.org
Web: www.hsp.org
Catalog: See website

Institutional, Private
Size: 20
Date Range: 1680–1821
Lend: No
Copy: See details below

Details: The Abraham H. Cassel Collection includes items relating to the Ephrata Cloister: hymnbooks; letter book (1755) of Conrad Beissel; collection of songs composed and arranged by Johannes Kelpius; and the death register of the cloister, 1728–1821. The remainder of the collection is comprised of religious tracts, hymnbooks, and schoolbooks. Many of the hymnals are illustrated.

Denominations: *German Seventh Day Baptist*

256. Lutheran Theological Seminary at Philadelphia
Krauth Memorial Library
7301 Germantown Ave.
Philadelphia, Pennsylvania 19119
Contact: Karl Krueger, Assistant Librarian
Ph: (215) 248-6330
Fax: (215) 248-6327
E-mail: kkrueger@ltsp.edu
Web: www.ltsp.edu/krauth
Catalog: See website

Institutional, Private
Size: 3,000
Date Range: 16th–present
Lend: See details below
Copy: See details below

Details: The library has 3,000 cataloged hymnals from collections of Luther Reed, C. P. Krauth, J. F. Ohl, J. A. Seiss, and the Hymn Society of America (duplicates culled pre-1950 from the Hymn Society's collection). Special strengths in German and Lutheran works from Reformation era on. Strong collection in liturgics. The Lutheran Archives Center in the library has early American Lutheran music manuscripts.

Will lend non-rare, nonfragile materials via interlibrary loan at standard interlibrary loan charges (see OCLC). In-house use available to any researcher. Open Monday–Friday 9 a.m.–5 p.m. year-round, 9 a.m.–10 p.m. during school terms.

Denominations: *Lutheran*

257. Presbyterian Historical Society
425 Lombard St.
Philadelphia, Pennsylvania 19147

Institutional, Private
Size: 1,400
Date Range: 17th–20th

Contact: Deputy Director
Ph: (215) 627-1852
Fax: (215) 627-0509
E-mail: refdesk@history.pcusa.org
Web: www.history.pcusa.org

Lend: No
Copy: See details below

Details: The collection includes several Issac Watts editions as well as Presbyterian and Reformed hymnals and tunebooks.

Closed-stacks repository. Requests for limited photocopying will be considered if it can be done without injury to the material.

Denominations: *Presbyterian, Reformed*

258. Pittsburgh Theological Seminary
Clifford E. Barbour Library
616 N. Highland Ave.
Pittsburgh, Pennsylvania 15206
Contact: Anita Johnson, Head of Public Services
Ph: (412) 362-5610
Fax: (412) 362-2329
E-mail: ajohnson@pts.edu
Web: www.pts.edu/library.html

Institutional, Private
Size: 3,500
Date Range: 16th–20th
Lend: No
Copy: See details below

Details: James Warrington Hymnology Collection: James Warrington's second great collection was acquired in 1917 by Western Theological Seminary, which merged in 1960 with Pittsburgh Theological Seminary. Over 3,500 hymnals, psalters, and songbooks are cataloged and arranged chronologically from the sixteenth century to the twentieth century, with the majority in the nineteenth century (over 450 before 1820).

Photocopying limited by staff availability and condition of item. Open Monday–Friday 8:30 a.m.–4:30 p.m.

Denominations: *Presbyterian*

259. Reformed Presbyterian Theological Seminary
7418 Penn Ave.

Institutional, Private
Size: 300
Date Range: 16th–21st

Pittsburgh, Pennsylvania 15208
Contact: Thomas Reid, Librarian
Ph: (412) 731-8690
Fax: (412) 731-4834
E-mail: treid@rpts.edu
Web: www.rpts.edu/library.html

Lend: Yes
Copy: Yes

Details: 300 psalmbooks and books about psalmody, in many languages; most are U.S. imprints. Also recordings of psalms being sung a cappella.

Denominations: *Reformed Presbyterian*

260. University of Pittsburgh
Theodore M. Finney
Music Library
B30 Music Bldg.
Pittsburgh, Pennsylvania 15260
Contact: Music Librarian
Ph: (412) 624-4131
Fax: (412) 624-4180
E-mail: music@library.pitt.edu
Web: www.library.pitt.edu/libraries/music/music.html
Catalog: See website

Institutional, Public
Size: 858
Date Range: 19th–early 20th
Lend: No
Copy: Yes

Details: The library has 858 cataloged items, and an unspecified number of others waiting to be cataloged. Collection includes 20 pre-1820 U.S. imprints, 165 Sunday school songbooks, 161 gospel songbooks, 11 Anglican, 40 Church of England, 10 Lutheran, and 28 Orthodox hymnals. Also 11 hymnals in German.

Open to visitors and researchers Monday–Friday 8:30 a.m.–5 p.m.

Denominations: *Anglican, Lutheran, Orthodox*

261. Pennsylvania State University
Special Collections Library
104 Paterno Library
University Park, Pennsylvania
16802
Contact: Sandra Stelts,

Institutional, Public
Size: 107
Date Range: 18th–20th
Lend: Yes
Copy: Yes

Associate Curator of Rare Books & Manuscripts
Ph: (814) 863-1793
Fax: (814) 863-5318
E-mail: sks@psulias.psu.edu
Web: www.libraries.psu.edu/crsweb/speccol/spcoll.htm
Catalog: www.libraries.psu.edu

Details: Thirty-one tunebooks, 1780s–1870s. Twenty Pennsylvania imprints from the eighteenth century, and seventy-six from the nineteenth century.

262. American Baptist Historical Society
Valley Forge Archives Center
P.O. Box 851
Valley Forge, Pennsylvania 19482
Contact: Deborah Bingham Van Broekhoven, Executive Director
Ph: (610) 768-2378
Fax: (610) 768-2266
E-mail: Deborah.VanBroekhoven@abc-usa.org
Web: www.abc-usa.org/abhs/abhscollection.html

Institutional, Private
Size: 100
Date Range: 19th–20th
Lend: No
Copy: See details below

Details: The Historical Judson Press Collection includes 100 hymnals, in addition to all materials (1840–present) published by the American Baptist Publication Society.

Will copy depending on condition of item.

Denominations: *Baptist*

263. Dave Hunter, Kerry Mueller
210 Hillsboro Mills Ln.
Wallingford, Pennsylvania 19086
Ph: (610) 872-2859
E-mail: dhhunter@comcast.net

Individual
Size: 350
Date Range: 19th–20th
Lend: No
Copy: Yes

Details: A WordPerfect list of hymnals is available.

Denominations: *Unitarian, Unitarian Universalist, Universalist*

264. Lycoming College Library *Institutional, Private*
Central Pennsylvania Conference of the United Methodist Church
United Methodist Archives
Williamsport, Pennsylvania 17701
Contact: Milton Loyer, Archivist
Ph: (570) 321-4088
E-mail: loyer@lycoming.edu
Web: www.lycoming.edu/dept/umarch

Size: 1,000
Date Range: 19th–20th
Lend: No
Copy: Yes

Details: Over 500 gospel songbooks 1850–1930. Nearly complete denominational collections for Evangelical Association, Methodist Episcopal, and United Brethren in Christ.

Denominations: *Evangelical Association, Methodist Episcopal, United Brethren in Christ*

265. David B. Whitney *Individual*
8 Ellen Dr. K.T.
Wyoming, Pennsylvania 18644
Ph: (570) 696-2218

Date Range: 16th–20th
Lend: See details below
Copy: See details below

Details: Strong in named tunes, nineteenth-century (especially oblongs), British, sacred dance, temperance. Wide range of musical styles and of theology; French, German, Spanish, and Welsh languages.

Looking to place collection in institution. Seeking exchanges, purchases, and gifts of books, leaflets, manuscripts, audio recordings, etc. of hymns, tunes, other sacred music and metrical or rhymed poetry, sacred dance, and hymn or hymntune indexes (several pages listing available 1800s duplicates sent on request). Seeking original writing of hymns, tunes, sacred music, and sacred choreography. Lending or copying will be considered. Visits by appointment.

Denominations: *Baptist, Brethren, Catholic, Congregational, Episcopal, Judaic, Lutheran, Mennonite, Methodist, Moravian, Orthodox, Presbyterian, Reformed, Unitarian, Universalist*

Rhode Island

266. Brown University
John Carter Brown Library
Box 1894
Providence, Rhode Island 02912
Contact: Reference Librarian
Ph: (401) 863-1263
Fax: (401) 863-3477
E-mail: JCBL_Information@Brown.edu
Web: www.jcbl.org

Institutional, Private
Size: 200
Date Range: pre-1825
Lend: No
Copy: See details below

Details: Rare book library which collects printed materials related to the western hemisphere (North America, South America, Mexico and Caribbean) pre-ca. 1825.

No photocopying, but microfilm available for whole pieces (no excerpts).

Many hymnals are only in the card catalog, so a visit to the library is essential to know the full scope of holdings.

267. Brown University
John Hay Library
Box A
Providence, Rhode Island 02912
Contact: Head Librarian, Special Collections
Ph: (401) 863-1514
Fax: (401) 863-2093
E-mail: hay@brown.edu
Web: www.brown.edu/Facilities/University_Library
Catalog: library.brown.edu

Institutional, Private
Size: 4,850
Date Range: 17th–20th
Lend: See details below
Copy: See details below

Details: The library has 3,500 hymnals with music, 1,350 words-only. Hymnals of American and Canadian imprint, dating from the seventeenth century to the present day. All denominations included. Collection features an interesting selection of Pennsylvania German imprints; twentieth-century hymnals from small, fundamentalist groups in the West, South, and Midwest; shape-note hymnals; sheet music for hymns, Christmas music, and the like are included in an allied sheet music collection.

Lend: individual decisions based on condition, to the custody of other special collections facilities.

Copy: individual decisions based on condition and copyright status. Microfilm rather than photocopy supplied for entire volumes requested.

268. Providence Public Library
225 Washington St.
Providence, Rhode Island 02903
Contact: Margaret Chevian, Art & Music Specialist
Ph: (401) 455-8088
Fax: (401) 455-8013
E-mail: mchevian@provlib.org
Web: www.provlib.org
Catalog: seq.clan.lib.ri.us

Institutional, Public
Size: 500
Date Range: late 19th–20th
Lend: Yes
Copy: Yes

Details: Most materials can be borrowed by Rhode Island residents with library card; interlibrary loan otherwise.

South Carolina

269. Lutheran Theological Southern Seminary
Lineberger Memorial Library
4201 N. Main St.
Columbia, South Carolina 29203
Contact: Lynn Feider, Director
Ph: (803) 786-5150
E-mail: LFeider@ltss.edu
Web: www.ltss.edu/library.html
Catalog: See website

Institutional, Private
Size: 600
Date Range: 18th–20th
Lend: See details below
Copy: No

Details: The library has a good collection of Lutheran hymnals.

Will loan materials depending on age and physical condition.

Denominations: *Episcopal, Lutheran, Methodist*

270. Erskine Theological Seminary
McCain Library

Institutional, Private
Size: 580

1 Depot St.
Due West, South Carolina 29639
Contact: Reference Librarian
Ph: (864) 379-8898
Fax: (864) 379-2900
E-mail: library@erskine.edu
Web: www.erskine.edu/library
Catalog: scotty.erskine.edu

Date Range: 19th–20th
Lend: See details below
Copy: See details below

Details: Arthur C. Bridges Hymnal Collection: Presbyterian hymnals strongly represented, but there are many Baptist, Methodist, and Episcopal/Church of England hymnals as well. Hymnals from the Presbyterian Church in Scotland (Church of Scotland) and Presbyterian Church in Ireland are also in the collection. There are also many nondenominational hymnals, and many words-only hymnals. The collection contains shape-note hymnals and a variety of psalters.

Most can be on loan through interlibrary loan. Requests through interlibrary loan cover photocopies.

Denominations: *Anglican, Baptist, Episcopal, Methodist, nondenominational, Presbyterian*

271. Bob Jones University
J. S. Mack Library
Greenville, South Carolina 29614
Contact: Special Collections Librarian
Ph: (864) 242-5100
Fax: (864) 232-1729
E-mail: library@bju.edu
Web: www2.bju.edu/resources/library

Institutional, Private
Size: 800
Date Range: 1739–1993
Lend: No
Copy: See details below

Details: American Hymnody Collection: This collection traces the development of hymnody in America from colonial days to the present. The collection consists of hymnals used (but not necessarily published) in the United States. The collection began in 1995 shortly after the university purchased a group of older American hymnals and songbooks. Since then, donations have been received from across the country, as well as from foreign countries, to help expand the collection. The collection currently numbers about 800 volumes and spans 1739–1993. Online catalog; catalog records are not available from outside the library.

Copying depends on the condition of the item.

272. Wofford College — *Institutional, Private*
Sandor Teszler Library
429 N. Church St.
Spartanburg, South Carolina 29303
Contact: Oakley H. Coburn, Dean of the Library
Ph: (864) 597-4300
Fax: (864) 597-4329
E-mail: coburnoh@wofford.edu
Web: www.wofford.edu/sandorteszlerlibrary

Size: 1,700
Date Range: 19th–20th
Lend: No
Copy: See details below

Details: Haynes-Brown Hymnal Collection: Approximately 1,700 nineteenth- and twentieth-century American hymnals and songbooks, including gospel and Southern folk with some words-only; collected mostly by Pierce Gault. Will photocopy or scan if condition permits. Cataloging in process.

Tennessee

273. Lee University — *Institutional, Private*
Pentecostal Resource Center
260 11th St. NE
Cleveland, Tennessee 37311
Contact: Director
Ph: (423) 614-8576
Fax: (423) 614-8555
E-mail: dixon_research@leeuniversity.edu
Web: www.leeuniversity.edu/library/dixon

Date Range: 20th
Lend: No
Copy: See details below

Details: James D. Vaughan Music Publisher Collection: Uncataloged hymnals of Southern publishers, mostly seven-shape, some four-shape.

Tennessee Music & Printing Co. Collection: The Hall, Parris-Denson, George W. Sebran, A. J. Showalter, and James D. Vaughan companies held publication rights to these materials—

which include twenty thousand items dating back to 1900—prior to their acquisition by this collection. Many of the items are paperback shape-note tunebooks.

Open to visitors and researchers Monday–Friday 8 a.m.–5 p.m.

Denominations: *Church of God*

274. Pathway Press [1988] *Institutional, Private*
1080 Montgomery Ave.
Cleveland, Tennessee 37311
Ph: (800) 553-8506
Fax: (800) 546-7590
E-mail: info@pathwaypress.org
Web: www.pathwaypress.org

Details: Uncataloged hymnals of Southern publications, mostly seven-shape, some four-shape. Many paperbacks.

Denominations: *Church of God*

275. Knox County Public Library System *Institutional, Public*
314 W. Clinch Ave.
Knoxville, Tennessee 37902-2313
Contact: Manager
Ph: (865) 215-8808
Fax: (865) 215-8810
E-mail: kcplmccl@kornet.org
Web: www.knoxlib.org
Size: 120
Date Range: 18th–early 20th
Lend: No
Copy: See details below

Details: George Pullen Jackson and Calvin M. McClung Historical Collections: The George Pullen Jackson Collection dates from the late eighteenth to the early twentieth century. Of particular interest are seventy-one volumes of sacred music and instruction books. See website for more details on the McClung Collection.

Might copy some small parts of books, but not whole volumes, unless an institution is willing to bear the expense of microfilming. All volumes are cataloged on OCLC. The volumes are of local and regional interest, emphasizing shape-note and locally published materials.

276. James D. Vaughan Museum *Insitutional, Private*
P.O. Box 607
Lawrenceburg, Tennessee 38464
Contact: Tom Crews, Curator
Ph: (800) 547-6500
E-mail: topcat815@lorettotel.net
Web: members.tripod.com/vaughanmuseum

Size: 100
Date Range: 20th
Lend: No
Copy: Yes

Details: About 100 paperback songbooks published by James D. Vaughan.

Open Monday–Friday, 9 a.m.–11 a.m., 12:30 p.m.–3 p.m., and Saturdays by appointment.

277. University of Memphis *Institutional, Public*
Special Collections
University of Memphis Libraries
Memphis, Tennessee 38152-3250
Contact: Ed Frank, Curator
Ph: (901) 678-2210
E-mail: efrank@memphis.edu
Web: www.lib.memphis.edu/speccoll.htm

Size: 100
Date Range: 19th–20th
Lend: See details below
Copy: Yes

Details: Mississippi Valley Collection: About 100 cataloged hymnals, emphasis on Southern denominations and nineteenth-century tunebooks. Two Danish hymnals.

Open to visitors and researchers. Will photocopy and send on interlibrary loan forms.

278. Country Music Hall of Fame *Institutional, Private*
Museum Library
222 5th St. S.
Nashville, Tennessee 37203
Contact: Dawn Oberg,
Reference Librarian
Ph: (615) 416-2036
Fax: (615) 255-2245

Size: 200
Date Range: 19th–mid-20th
Lend: No
Copy: Yes

E-mail: doberg@countrymusichalloffame.com
Web: www.countrymusichalloffame.org/museum/lib

Details: Large songbook and sheet music collection, of which hymnals and sacred songs are a small part. Hymnals are mostly twentieth-century Protestant, but include shape-note songbooks and songs for tent and revival meetings. Also have sheet music for sacred songs. Many hymnals published by Vaughan and Stamps. Also have a large sound-recording collection, and many sacred songs sung by country and/or Southern gospel artists.

Denominations: *Baptist*

279. David Lipscomb University
Beaman Library
3901 Granny White Pike
Nashville, Tennessee 37204-3951
Contact: Marie P. Byers, Special Collections Librarian
Ph: (615) 279-5719
Fax: (615) 296-1807
E-mail: Marie.Byers@lipscomb.edu
Web: library.lipscomb.edu
Catalog: See website

Institutional, Private
Size: 2,000
Date Range: 18th–21st
Lend: No
Copy: Yes

Details: Ernie R. Bailey Hymnology Collection: Hymnals from different groups, nondenominational and interdenominational; reference books; handbooks to hymnals, concordances of church music, and histories of hymnology; several hymnology journals; predominantly English, but also includes hymnals in French, German, Italian, Spanish, and Swedish, among others. Oldest book is a 1732 French psalter. A card file lists hymnals by title, by denomination, and by special features; also includes a list of reference books.

Includes hymnals from the collection of Tom Fettke.

Special Collections is open Monday–Friday 1–4 p.m. or by appointment.

Denominations: *interdenominational, nondenominational*

280. Disciples of Christ Historical Society
Library & Archives
1101 19th Ave. S.
Nashville, Tennessee 37212-2196
Ph: (615) 327-1444
Fax: (615) 327-1445
E-mail: mail@dishistsoc.org
Web: users.aol.com/dishistsoc

Institutional, Private
Size: 400
Date Range: 19th–20th
Lend: See details below
Copy: Yes

Details: Some of the hymnals are words-only.

Open to visitors and members Monday–Friday 8 a.m.–4:30 p.m. Will photocopy for visitors, but lend only to libraries and members. Will consider exchange.

Denominations: *Christian Church (Disciples of Christ), Christian Churches and Churches of Christ, Churches of Christ*

281. LifeWay Christian Resources of the Southern Baptist Convention
E. C. Dargan Research Library
127 9th Ave. N.
Nashville, Tennessee 37234-0142
Contact: Librarian
Ph: (615) 251-2126
Fax: (615) 251-2176
E-mail: library@lifeway.com
Web: divinity.library.vanderbilt.edu/ttla/Libraries/dargan.htm

Institutional, Private
Size: 250
Date Range: 20th
Lend: See details below
Copy: See details below

Details: Hymnals used by Baptists and published by Baptists. Includes Press Collection for Convention Press, Broadman and Holman, LifeWay Press. Most are twentieth-century.

Denominations: *Baptist*

282. Southern Baptist Historical Library and Archives
901 Commerce St., #400
Nashville, Tennessee 37203

Institutional, Private
Size: 600
Date Range: 18th–20th
Lend: No

Contact: Bill Sumners, Director **Copy:** Yes
Ph: (615) 244-0344
Fax: (615) 782-4821
E-mail: bill@sbhla.org
Web: www.sbhla.org

Details: Collection includes about 250 print copies of mostly Baptist hymnals and about 350 on microfilm. Primarily from the nineteenth and twentieth centuries with some earlier songbooks. Microfilm can be purchased.

Denominations: *Baptist*

283. United Methodist Publishing House [1988] *Institutional, Private*
Size: 1,200
Library
201 8th Ave. S.
P.O. Box 801
Nashville, Tennessee 37202-0801
Ph: (615) 749-6000
Web: www.umph.org

Details: Over 1,200 cataloged Methodist hymnals in the publisher's library.

Denominations: *Methodist*

284. Vanderbilt University *Institutional, Private*
Divinity Library
419 21st Ave. South
Nashville, Tennessee 37240-0007
Size: 350
Date Range: 18th–20th
Lend: No
Copy: See details below
Contact: Bill Hook, Director
Ph: (615) 322-2865
Fax: (615) 343-2918
E-mail: hook@library.vanderbilt.edu
Web: divinity.library.vanderbilt.edu
Catalog: See website

Details: Tillett Hymnody Collection: Collection donated to the library by Dean Tillett, from his personal library. Other than historical artifacts of the building of the divinity library, modern hymnody purchases (modest) are primarily the province of the music library now. Most of the collection dates from the late nineteenth and early twentieth centuries.

Online records available: All should be cataloged in ACORN, accessible on the web. Copying on a limited scale and depends on condition of item.

285. Carlton R. Young
2119 32nd Ave. S.
Nashville, Tennessee 37212
E-mail: musam@aol.com

Individual
Size: 700
Date Range: 18th–20th
Lend: No
Copy: No

Details: British American hymnals, tunebooks, and songbooks.

Denominations: *Methodist*

286. University of the South [1988]
Jessie Ball duPont Library
735 University Ave.
Sewanee, Tennessee 37383-1000
Ph: (931) 598-1265
Fax: (931) 598-1702
Web: library.sewanee.edu

Institutional, Private
Size: 150
Date Range: 19th

Details: Among the holdings are Episcopal hymnals dating from the 1840s.

Denominations: *Episcopal*

Texas

287. Abilene Christian University
Milliken Special Collections
Margaret and Herman Brown Library
Box 29208
Abilene, Texas 79699
Contact: Erma Jean Loveland, Special Collections Librarian
Ph: (915) 674-2538

Institutional, Private
Size: 451
Date Range: 1854–present
Lend: No
Copy: See details below

E-mail: lovelande@acu.edu
Web: www.acu.edu/academics/library/cfm
Catalog: See website

Details: Austin Taylor Hymnbook Collection: The nucleus of the collection was a 451-book collection given by the Austin Taylor children. To this have been added hymnals of the Restoration Movement, particularly the paperback American revival hymnals. Collection includes hymnals published by the Firm Foundation and Gospel Advocate, as well as by Austin Taylor and Alexander Campbell. Catalog records available on ALCON, Abilene Library Consortium Online.

Callie Faye Milliken Special Collections also has twenty-six original song manuscripts with accompanying explanatory notes and words of Tillit S. Teddlie (1885–1987). Finding aids for the manuscript collection cannot be accessed outside of the Brown Library.

Copying depends on the age and condition of the item.

Denominations: *Christian Church (Disciples of Christ), Christian Churches and Churches of Christ, Churches of Christ*

288. Hardin-Simmons University
Smith Music Library
P.O. Box 16230
Abilene, Texas 79698-6230
Contact: Murl Sickbert, Music Librarian
Ph: (915) 670-1433
Fax: (915) 677-8351
E-mail: sickbert@hsutx.edu
Web: rupert.alc.org/library
Catalog: See website

Institutional, Private
Size: 1,150
Date Range: 17th–early 20th
Lend: No
Copy: Yes

Details: The Thurman Lee and Lucialis Morrison Collection of Early American Hymnody was acquired for the Smith Music Library by the HSU School of Music Foundation in 1991. Thurman Morrison was a long-time professor of piano and music history at Hardin-Simmons. The collection of more that 1,000 items spans from the mid-seventeenth century to the early twentieth century. The earliest item in the collection is a Sternhold and Hopkins psalter bound with Holy Bible dated 1647. Several collections of eighteenth-century psalmody are also a part of the collection and a few items from the First New England School, notably a tune-book apparently owned by William Billings's daughter. The bulk of the collection consists of tunebooks from the nineteenth-century New England reformers: Lowell Mason, George Webb, William Bradbury, etc. This includes a number of Sunday school collections. Much of Morrison's collecting was done during vacations in New England, so the collection is oriented toward the round-note tradition. Very few examples of shape-note hymnody. The collection extends to the early period of gospel hymnody through to Stamps Baxter gospel collections of the early twentieth century. The Morrison Collection continues to be cataloged and is therefore only partially accessible through the Abilene Library Consortium (ALCON) database.

The Sims Hymnal Collection started as a gift from W. Hines Sims, an HSU alumnus and editor of the 1956 edition of the *Baptist Hymnal*. His donation was a core collection of denominational hymnals from the first half of the twentieth century. The library has continued to add hymnals from all denominations published since 1960 as well as hymnal companions and other hymnological reference works. The collection is fully accessible through the Abilene Library Consortium (ALCON) database.

289. Episcopal Church — *Institutional, Private*

Archives of the Episcopal Church
P.O. Box 2247
606 Rathervue Place
Austin, Texas 78768
Contact: Canonical Archivist
Ph: (512) 472-6816
Fax: (512) 480-0437
E-mail: research@episcopalarchives.org
Web: www.episcopalarchives.org

Size: 400
Date Range: 19th–20th
Lend: No
Copy: See details below

Details: Fragile books not copied.

Denominations: *Episcopal*

290. University of Texas at Austin
Harry Ransom Humanities Research Center
P.O. Box 7219
Austin, Texas 78713-7219
Contact: Books Collection, Reference Librarian
Ph: (512) 471-9119
Fax: (512) 471-2899
E-mail: reference@hrc.utexas.edu
Web: www.hrc.utexas.edu
Catalog: See website

Institutional, Public
Size: 250
Date Range: 19th–20th
Lend: No
Copy: Yes

Details: Katharine Diehl Hymnal Collection, 130 titles; hymnal collection (uncataloged), 117 titles.

291. Dallas Theological Seminary [1988]
Moser Library
3909 Swiss Ave.
Dallas, Texas 75204
Ph: (800) 992-0998 or (214) 824-3094
Fax: (214) 841-3664
Web: www.dts.edu

Institutional, Private
Size: 250
Date Range: 1880–present

Details: The library has 250 hymnals representing many denominations.

292. Southern Methodist University
Bridwell Library
Center for Methodist Studies
P.O. Box 750476
Dallas, Texas 75275-0476
Contact: Director, Center for Methodist Studies
Ph: (214) 768-2363
Fax: (214) 768-4295
E-mail: bridcms@mail.smu.edu
Web: www2.smu.edu/bridwell
Catalog: See website

Institutional, Private
Size: 2,000
Date Range: 18th–20th
Lend: No
Copy: See details below

Details: Ninety percent of the collection is Methodist-related, consisting of hymnals and papers dealing with the editing and publishing of these hymnals. The remaining ten percent are gospel hymnals, hymnals of other denominations, and general hymnals.

Official hymnals of the Methodist Episcopal Church; Methodist Episcopal Church, South; Methodist Protestant Church; Methodist Church (United States); United Methodist Church (United States); Wesleyan Methodist Church (Great Britain); hymnals of John and Charles Wesley before 1791 (144).

The Alfredo and Clotilde Nanez Hispanic Church Music Collection consists of about 200 hymnals, choirbooks, *cancioneros,** song sheets, and manuscript worksheets (manuscript sheets with translations of English hymns into Spanish with notes).

**Cancioneros* are small paperback booklets in Spanish. There are usually ten to thirty songs in one volume, often privately or locally printed.

Archival Material:
Papers related to the editing of the 1935 *Methodist Hymnal*, 1966 *Methodist Hymnal,* and *Companion to the Hymnal;* 1989 *United Methodist Hymnal* and the 1993 *Companion to the United Methodist Hymnal.*

Robert G. McCutchan, ed. of the 1935 *Methodist Hymnal;* Fred D. Gealy, ed. of the *Companion* of the 1966 *Methodist Hymnal;* Carlton R. Young, ed. of the 1966 *Methodist Hymnal*, 1989 *United Methodist Hymnal,* and the 1993 *Companion to the United Methodist Hymnal;* Roger Deschner Papers pertaining to the Hymnal Revision Committee and his files on Music and the Wesleys, ethnic hymns, and worship resources.

Some copying of printed hymnals is permitted, but most copying is done by library staff. Copying of archival material is done by library staff. Policies are flexible and there are always exceptions.

Denominations: *Methodist Church, Methodist Episcopal, Methodist Episcopal Church (South), Methodist Protestant, United Methodist, Wesleyan Methodist (Great Britain)*

293. Carry Edward Spann
Dallas Baptist University
3000 Mountain Creek Pkwy.
Dallas, Texas 75211
Ph: (214) 333-5316
Fax: (214) 333-6804
E-mail: ed@dbu.edu

Individual
Size: 200
Date Range: 19th–21st

Details: Hymnals in Chinese, English, Korean, Portuguese, Russian, Spanish, Vietnamese, etc. A variety of denominations are represented as well as nondenominational hymnals. The collection also includes all standard hymnology books, including most of Erik Routley's writings. Also an extensive section on hymn story books and general books on church music, both standard and unique. Old hymnals are not in good shape but do include Sankey's *Sacred Songs and Solos*. Includes more than fifty shape-note songbooks, and all "Singspiration" series. Also many books on aesthetics of music, music theory, and history of music.

This collection has been acquired over almost fifty years and many sources are used in teaching a hymnology course.

Denominations: *nondenominational*

294. Southwestern Baptist Theological Seminary
Kathryn Sullivan Bowld Music Library
P.O. Box 22000-D4
Ft. Worth, Texas 76122-0390
Contact: Fang-Lan Hsieh, Music Librarian
Ph: (817) 923-1921
Fax: (817) 921-8762
E-mail: fhsieh@lib.swbts.edu
Web: www.swbts.edu/libraries
Catalog: draweb2.swbts.edu

Institutional, Private
Size: 8,000
Date Range: 16th–20th
Lend: See details below
Copy: Yes

Details: The George C. Stebbins Collection contains over 1,100 items and includes hymnals, sacred songbooks, histories, biographies, and scrapbooks related to American hymnody. Although the collection contains materials dating from the middle of the eighteenth century to the middle of the twentieth century, the essence of the collection is gospel hymnody of the revivalistic period of the nineteenth century. Assembled mostly by the Rev. James Benjamin Clayton, whose desire was "to include all, and exclude none, of the varied manifestations of evangelistic song, thus furnishing an ample and unbiased mass of material for the study of the origins, development, and distribution of the Gospel hymn," the collection was housed at the National Cathedral in Washington, D.C., beginning in 1930. Through the efforts of Dr. William J. Reynolds and Dr. Carl R. Wrotenbery, the collection was transferred to Southwestern Baptist Theological Seminary in 1988 and is now housed in the Robert S. Douglass Treasure Room inside the Kathryn Sullivan Bowld Music Library. The collection also includes items from around the world and in various languages.

To view the titles in the Stebbins Collection, access the SWBTS Library Online Catalog, and use "Stebbins Collection" (without the quotation marks) as the title.

Many items in the collection are of a fragile nature and must be handled with care. Items that are not found in the Treasure Room may be loaned through interlibrary loan. Will also copy materials.

Denominations: *Baptist*

295. Southwestern University
A. Frank Smith, Jr. Library
P.O. Box 770
Georgetown, Texas 78727-0770
Contact: Kathryn Stallard,
Head of Special Collections
Ph: (512) 863-1563
E-mail: stallark@southwestern.edu
Web: www.southwestern.edu/library

Institutional, Private
Size: 300
Date Range: 1594–present
Lend: See details below
Copy: See details below

Details: Meyer Hymnal Collection: Southwestern University's collection of hymnals and related works includes over 300 hymnals. A significant number of the hymnals are Methodist or Methodist Episcopal, but many other denominations are represented, including Baptist, Presbyterian, Christian Science, and Mormon. At least one African Methodist Episcopal hymnal (1946) is in the collection, as well as works of the Primitive Methodist sect of England. The earliest work is a single leaf from the *Psalter of the Pilgrim Fathers* (1594). The earliest complete hymnal is the Wesleys' *Hymns and Sacred Poems* (London: printed by W. Strahan; and sold by James Hutton, bookseller . . . and at Mr. Bray's, 1739). Another eighteenth-century title is *The Collection of Hymns Sung in the Countess of Huntingdon's Chapels* (Bath: W. Gye, 1774). Most hymnals, however, are from the nineteenth and early twentieth century. Children's hymnals, many revival and camp-meeting hymnals, and psalters (including Isaac Watts's) are also found in the collection. Some hymnals are from the Jackson-Greenwood Collection or the university's collection of Methodist materials. The collection holds numerous English-language hymnals produced by and for the Methodist Church. There is also a work in the Delaware language. Approximately fifteen hymnals are in German and a few are in other languages.

Decisions to loan or copy are determined by rarity and condition of item.

Denominations: *African Methodist Episcopal, Baptist, Christian Science, Church of Jesus Christ of Latter-day Saints, Methodist, Methodist Episcopal, Presbyterian, Primitive Methodist*

296. David G. Nussman
5844 Valley Forge Dr.
Houston, Texas 77057
Ph: (713) 784-2286

Individual
Size: 3,000
Date Range: 1810–20th
Lend: See details below
Copy: Yes

Details: Isaac Watts, nineteenth-century tunebooks (from 1810); includes books about hymnology. United Church of Christ holdings include: United Church of Christ, Congregational, Evangelical Synod, Reformed Church in the United States, and a few Christian Connexion.

Willing to lend materials under unusual circumstances. Willing to copy limited materials for cost.

Denominations: *Christian Connexion, Congregational, Evangelical Synod, Reformed Church in the United States, Unitarian, United Church of Christ*

297. Laurie Gruenbeck
3103 Saunders Ave.
San Antonio, Texas 78207
Ph: (210) 434-8938

Individual
Size: 480
Date Range: mid-19th–21st
Lend: No
Copy: Yes

Details: The collection includes 420 anthologies and hymnals, 60 indexes, histories, etc.; 500 recordings, mainly records, some cassettes and CDs. Hymnals range from mid-1800s–2000. There are some copies or reprints of older publications. Some indexing in French, German, Hungarian, Polish, and Spanish. Catholic and Protestant holdings.

Denominations: *Catholic*

298. Baylor University
Crouch Fine Arts Library
P.O. Box 97148
Waco, Texas 76798
Contact: Sha Towers,
Public Services Supervisor
Ph: (254) 710-6673
Fax: (254) 710-3116
E-mail: Sha_Towers@baylor.edu
Web: www.baylor.edu/Library/FineArts
Catalog: bearcat.baylor.edu

Institutional, Private
Size: 1,150
Date Range: 16th–20th
Lend: Yes
Copy: Yes

Details: Travis and Margaret Johnson Collection: The collection includes hymnals in a number of languages representing approximately forty religious groups or denominations. The circulating hymnal collection contains approximately 400 nineteenth-

and twentieth-century hymnals. Approximately 750 hymnals are in various noncirculating special collections. American oblong tunebooks; shape-note hymnody; gospel hymnody; camp-meeting and revival hymnody; Sunday school movement. No formal collection development policy, but try to collect as broadly and currently as possible to complement Baylor's Church Music Studies program. Hymnals included in the rare and special collections are also represented in John Minnear, *An Annotated Catalogue of the Rare Music in the Baylor University Library* (Master's thesis, Baylor University, 1963) and supplements which followed in 1969, 1972, and 1980.

In fall 2002, Baylor acquired the hymnal collection of Harry Eskew. This collection includes 1,850 hymnals and tunebooks related to shape-note tradition, early Sunday school and gospel hymn collections. Rare items include a first edition of William Walker's *Southern Harmony* (1835) and Walker's *Fruits and Flowers* (1873). Dates of publication range from the eighteenth to twenty-first centuries, and includes a number of Baptist titles.

Denominations: *Baptist*

Utah

299. Brigham Young University — *Institutional, Private*

L. Tom Perry Special Collections
1130 HBLL
P.O. Box 26835
Provo, Utah 84602-6835
Contact: Larry Draper,
Special Collections Librarian
Ph: (801) 378-6372
E-mail: Larry_Draper@byu.edu
Web: www.lib.byu.edu/hbll

Size: 250
Date Range: 19th–20th
Lend: No
Copy: No

Details: Mormon hymnals from the earliest (1835) to the present in English and various non-English languages; noncirculating.

Hours: Monday, Tuesday, Thursday, Friday 8 a.m.–5 p.m.; Wednesday 8 a.m.–9 p.m.; Saturday 10 a.m.–5 p.m.

Denominations: *Church of Jesus Christ of Latter-day Saints*

300. Church of Jesus Christ of Latter-day Saints
Church History Library
50 E. North Temple St.
Salt Lake City, Utah 84150-3800
Contact: Christine Cox, Director
Ph: (801) 240-2745
Fax: (801) 240-1845

Institutional, Public
Size: 500
Date Range: 1835–present
Lend: No
Copy: See details below

Details: The library has 500 cataloged hymnals, representing a rather complete collection of the Latter-day Saints hymnals from 1835, in several languages. Also, some non-LDS hymnals, including a few early Presbyterian and Methodist hymnals.

Limited photocopying but will not mail books. Will not copy entire works unless they are under 100 pages; will follow copyright laws.

Denominations: *Church of Jesus Christ of Latter-day Saints, Methodist, Presbyterian*

301. University of Utah
J. Willard Marriott Library
295 South 1500 East
Salt Lake City, Utah 84112
Contact: Gregory C. Thompson, Special Collections
Ph: (801) 581-8046
Fax: (801) 585-3976
E-mail: gthompso@library.utah.edu
Web: www.lib.utah.edu

Institutional, Public
Size: 200
Date Range: 18th–20th
Lend: No
Copy: See details below

Details: The library has 200 hymnals representing the Church of Jesus Christ of Latter-day Saints.

Will copy some materials depending on copyright and condition of item.

Denominations: *Church of Jesus Christ of Latter-day Saints*

302. Utah State Historical Society
300 Rio Grande
Salt Lake City, Utah 84101-1182
Contact: Collections Coordinator
Ph: (801) 533-3574
Fax: (801) 533-3504
E-mail: ushs@history.state.ut.us
Web: www.history.utah.org

Institutional, Public
Size: 50
Date Range: 1850–1980
Lend: No
Copy: Yes

Details: Hymnals represent the Church of Jesus Christ of Latter-day Saints and Reorganized Church of Jesus Christ of Latter-day Saints (Community of Christ).

Denominations: *Church of Jesus Christ of Latter-day Saints, Community of Christ*

Vermont

303. Vermont Historical Society [1988]
60 Washington St.
Barre, Vermont 05641
E-mail: vhs@vhs.state.vt.us
Web: www.state.vt.us/vhs

Institutional, Private
Size: 68
Date Range: 19th–20th

Details: Vermontiana Collection: Includes sixty-eight cataloged hymnals of which fifty-five are words-only. Emphasis on Methodist and Universalist items, mostly nineteenth-century.

Denominations: *Methodist, Universalist*

304. Middlebury College
Ethnomusicology Archives
Music Library
72 Porter Field Rd.
Middlebury, Vermont 05753
Contact: Terry Simpkins, Archives Librarian
Ph: (802) 443-5045
Fax: (802) 443-2057
E-mail: tsimpkin@middlebury.edu
Web: www.middlebury.edu/~lib/musiclib/musiclib.html

Institutional, Private
Size: 125
Date Range: 19th–20th
Lend: No
Copy: See details below

Details: Copying depends on age/condition of the item and number of pages requested.

305. Thetford Historical Society
P.O. Box 33
2274 Route 113
Thetford, Vermont 05074-0033
Contact: Charles Latham, President and Librarian
Ph: (802) 785-2068
Web: www.vmga.org/orange/thetfordhs.html

Institutional, Private
Size: 300
Date Range: 19th
Lend: No
Copy: Yes

Details: Charles W. Hughes Collection: Hughes (1900–1998) was coauthor of *American Hymns Old and New* (New York: Columbia University Press, 1980). He left the Historical Society his collection.

306. Woodstock Historical Library
John Cotton Dana Library
26 Elm St.
Woodstock, Vermont 05091
Contact: Don Wickman
Ph: (802) 457-1822
Fax: (802) 457-2811
E-mail: whs@sover.net
Web: www.vmga.org/windsor/woodhs.html

Institutional, Private
Size: 30
Date Range: 18th–19th
Lend: Yes
Copy: See details below

Details: One copy of an eighteenth-century hymnal, twenty assorted nineteenth-century hymnals, nine volumes of Watts (nineteenth-century printings).

Virginia

307. Randolph-Macon College
McGraw-Page Library
305 Henry St.
Ashland, Virginia 23005
Contact: Nancy Newins, Head of Reference
Ph: (804) 752-4718
Fax: (804) 752-7345
E-mail: nnewins@rmc.edu

Institutional, Private
Size: 3,500
Date Range: 18th–20th
Lend: No

Web: www.rmc.edu/library

Details: The Methodist Collection has approximately fifty Methodist hymnals dating back to the 1770s. These can be viewed by appointment only.

Denominations: *Methodist*

308. Bridgewater College
Alexander Mack Memorial Library
E. College St.
Bridgewater, Virginia 22812
Contact: Ruth Greenawalt, Director
Ph: (540) 828-5410
Fax: (540) 828-5482
E-mail: rgreenaw@bridgewater.edu
Web: www.bridgewater.edu/departments/library
Catalog: See website

Institutional, Private
Size: 500
Date Range: 18th–20th
Lend: No
Copy: Yes

Details: Donald R. Hinks's Brethren Hymn Books and Hymnals: Over 300 Church of the Brethren hymnals and approximately 200 from other denominations.

Denominations: *Church of the Brethren*

309. University of Virginia [1988]
Music Library
Old Cabell Hall
Charlottesville, Virginia 22903
Contact: Music Librarian
Ph: (434) 924-7041
Fax: (434) 924-6033
E-mail: musiclib@virginia.edu
Web: www.lib.virginia.edu/MusicLib

Institutional, Public
Size: 225
Date Range: 17th–20th

Details: About 225 cataloged hymnals representing most denominations. Emphasis on Episcopal, English, and German hymnals. Also tunebooks and psalmbooks, including Ruebush and Kieffer imprints.

Notable holdings: Protestant Episcopal hymnal (1811); Confederate psalmbook (1862); nine editions of the *Bay Psalm Book* (1698–1773); John Cotton, *Singing of Psalmes* (London, 1647). These are housed in the Rare Book Room of the Alderman Library.

Denominations: *Episcopal*

310. Fairfax County Public Library
Fairfax City Regional Library
3915 Chain Bridge Rd.
Fairfax, Virginia 22030
Contact: Maggie Belsan
Ph: (703) 246-2281
E-mail: maggie.belsan@co.fairfax.va.us
Web: www.co.fairfax.va.us/library
Catalog: fcplcat.co.fairfax.va.us

Institutional, Public
Size: 55
Date Range: 20th
Lend: Yes
Copy: Yes

Details: Collection of hymnals of various denominations.

311. Eastern Mennonite University
Menno Simons Historical Library
1200 Park Rd.
Harrisonburg, Virginia 22802
Contact: Lois B. Bowman, Historical Library Director
Ph: (540) 432-4178
Fax: (540) 432-4977
E-mail: bowmanlb@emu.edu
Web: www.emu.edu/library/histlib.html
Catalog: See website

Institutional, Private
Size: 1,500
Date Range: 16th–present
Lend: See details below
Copy: See details below

Details: Collection includes numerous shape-note hymnals, publications of Joseph Funk and the Ruebush-Kieffer Company. About 375 words-only.

Will lend duplicate materials that are designated for circulation. Will photocopy small portions (usually not entire books) if item is not too fragile. Open Monday–Friday 8 a.m.–noon, 1–5 p.m.

Denominations: *Amish, Mennonite*

312. Massanutten Regional Library
174 S. Main St.
Harrisonburg, Virginia 22801
Contact: Reference Librarian
Ph: (540) 434-4475
Fax: (540) 434-4382
E-mail: reference@mrlib.org
Web: www.mrlib.org

Institutional, Public
Size: 100
Date Range: 19th–20th
Lend: No
Copy: See details below

Details: 100 shape-note hymnals and music books, imprints of Ruebush & Kieffer and Joseph Funk.

Willing to copy from these materials, depending on condition.

313. Virginia Baptist Historical Society
P.O. Box 34
University of Richmond
Richmond, Virginia 23173
Contact: Research Assistant
Ph: (804) 289-8434
Web: www.baptistheritage.org

Institutional, Private
Size: 200
Date Range: 18th–20th
Lend: No
Copy: See details below

Details: Over 200 cataloged hymnals.

Open to visitors and researchers Monday–Friday 9 a.m.–4 p.m. by appointment. Will consider exchange.

Denominations: *Baptist*

314. Virginia Historical Society
P.O. Box 7311
428 N. Boulevard
Richmond, Virginia 23221
Contact: Frances Pollard, Assistant Director for Library Services
Ph: (804) 342-9677
Fax: (804) 355-2399
E-mail: reference@vahistorical.org
Web: www.vahistorical.org

Institutional, Private
Size: 118
Date Range: 17th–20th
Lend: No

Details: Five undated, one seventeenth-century, ninety-one nineteenth-century, twenty-one twentieth-century, of which a total of seventy are Virginia imprints and eleven are Confederate imprints. Joseph Holladay (d. 1795) holograph psalmbook dated 1769.

315. Regent University
Library
1000 Regent University Dr.
Virginia Beach, Virginia 23464
Contact: Donald Gantz,
Special Collections Supervisor
Ph: (757) 226-4154
Fax: (757) 226-4167
E-mail: donagan@regent.edu
Web: www.regent.edu/lib
Catalog: See website

Institutional, Private
Size: 9,000
Date Range: 17th–20th
Lend: No
Copy: See details below

Details: Keith C. Clark Hymnology Collection: Purchased from Clark, retired professional U.S. Army musician, in 1982. Hymnals representing a variety of Christian traditions, American and European, and well-known works on hymnody. *With a Voice of Singing,* 2nd ed. (Virginia Beach, Va.: CBN University, 1989) is a selected bibliography of master works in the collection compiled by former curator Jack Ralston.

See also James C. Weaver, "The Keith C. Clark Hymnal Collection." *The Hymn* 52, no. 3 (July 2001): 46–47.

316. W. M. Enright
P.O. Box 44
Wattsville, Virginia 23483
Ph: (757) 824-4365
E-mail: maury@intercom.net

Individual
Size: 1,000
Date Range: 19th–20th
Lend: See details below

Details: Has multiple copies of some books in varying conditions. Small collections of duplicate titles for use with various church groups. Would be glad to trade extra copies of books. No catalog.

***Denominations:** Baptist, Methodist, Presbyterian*

317. James H. Laster
125 Garden Court
Winchester, Virginia 22601
Ph: (540) 662-4907
E-mail: jlaster@shentel.net

Individual
Size: 50
Date Range: 19th–20th
Lend: Yes
Copy: Yes

Details: The collection contains fifty uncataloged hymnals collected while doing research in Iranian indigenous hymnody. Some examples of "cut and paste" tunebooks created by missionaries for use in local churches.

Denominations: *Anglican, Presbyterian*

Washington

318. Washington State University
Holland Library
P.O. Box 645610
Pullman, Washington 99164-5610
Contact: Paula Elliot,
Reference Librarian
Ph: (509) 335-8126
Fax: (509) 335-1889
E-mail: elliotp@wsu.edu
Web: www.wsulibs.wsu.edu
Catalog: griffin.wsu.edu

Institutional, Public
Size: 50
Date Range: 19th–20th
Lend: Yes
Copy: No

Details: Mainstream general collection. Mostly donations, usual Protestant materials.

319. Seattle Pacific University
Library
3307 Third Ave. W.
Seattle, Washington 98119-1997
Contact: Natalee Vick,
Liaison for Fine Arts
Ph: (206) 281-2735
Fax: (206) 281-2936
E-mail: nvick@spu.edu
Web: www.spu.edu/depts/library
Catalog: deborah.spu.edu

Institutional, Private
Size: 350
Date Range: 19th–20th
Lend: See details below
Copy: See details below

Details: Emphasis on Methodist and Free Methodist materials.

Some materials may be borrowed or photocopied for other libraries. Please use OCLC interlibrary loan or an American Library Association interlibrary loan form.

Denominations: *Free Methodist, Methodist*

320. Seattle Public Library
Arts, Recreation & Literature
800 Pike St.
Seattle, Washington 98101
Contact: Arts Manager
Ph: (206) 386-4613
Fax: (206) 386-4616
E-mail: infospl@spl.org
Web: www.spl.org
Catalog: See website

Institutional, Public
Size: 134
Date Range: 19th–20th
Lend: See details below
Copy: See details below

Details: Several gospel hymnals, 1 cosmic chant book, 12 volumes praise songbooks; 134 volumes of which 107 are accessible through computer catalog; others in print catalog. Mainly four-part, some two-part, some melody-only. Collection includes 2 hymnals in German, and 1 each of Dakota, French-Canadian, Hawaiian, Japanese, Norwegian, and Polish. One Jewish hymnal. Eleven words-only hymnals include 1 in Cherokee, 1 Chinook, 1 Danish, 1 German, 1 Icelandic, 1 Kalispel, 3 Latin, and 1 Welsh.

Open to visitors and researchers Monday–Thursday 9 a.m.–9 p.m., Friday 10:30 a.m.–6 p.m., Saturday 9 a.m.–6 p.m., Sunday 1–5 p.m. Will loan some through interlibrary loan.

Note: Library will be in a new location in 2004.

Denominations: *Catholic, Judaic*

321. University of Washington [1988]
Music Library
113 Music Building
Box 353450
Seattle, Washington 98195-3450

Institutional, Public
Size: 250

Contact: Head Librarian
Ph: (206) 543-1168
E-mail: musiclib@u.washington.edu
Web: www.lib.washington.edu/music

Details: The library has 250 cataloged early American hymnals and tunebooks in the Hazel Gertrude Kinscella (1893–1960) Collection.

322. Gonzaga University
Jesuit Oregon Province Archives
Special Collections
Foley Center Library
Spokane, Washington 99258
Contact: Archives/Special Collections Librarian
Ph: (509) 323-3814
Fax: (509) 324-5904
E-mail: jopa@foley.gonzaga.edu
Web: www.foley.gonzaga.edu

Institutional, Private
Size: 30
Date Range: 19th–mid 20th
Lend: No
Copy: Yes

Details: Indian Languages Collection: Hymnals in Native American languages including Athabascan, Blackfeet/Piegan, Cheyenne, Chinook, Chippewa, Coeur d'Alene, Cree, Crow, Inupiaq, Kalispel, Kootenai, Koyukon/Ten'a, Lakota/Santee, Micmac, Nez Perce, Ojibwa, Salish, Seneca, Takudh/Tukkuthkutchin, Tsimshian, Yup'ik.

On-site use only. Some manuscripts available on microfilm.

Denominations: *Catholic*

West Virginia

323. Bethany College
T. W. Phillips Memorial Library
Archives & Special Collections
Bethany, West Virginia 26032
Contact: R. Jeanne Cobb, Archivist and Coordinator of Special Collections
Ph: (304) 829-7898

Institutional, Private
Size: 32
Date Range: 1832–1870
Lend: No

Fax: (304) 829-7333
E-mail: j.cobb@mail.bethanywv.edu
Web: info.bethany.wvnet.edu/library

Details: The Bethany College Archives includes the Center for Campbell Studies. The Center interacts with holdings of the Campbell Collection, the Religious Heritage Collection, the Rare Book Collection, the Robert Richardson Collection, the Pendleton Family Papers, the Richard Bruce Kenney Papers, the Hiram J. Lester, Jr. Papers, the Upper Ohio Valley Collection, and Bethany College Archives.

The collection includes many editions of *The Christian Hymnbook,* compiled by Alexander Campbell, founder of Bethany College. The earliest edition is from 1832.

Denominations: *Christian Church (Disciples of Christ)*

Wisconsin

324. Hoard Historical Museum
407 Merchants Ave.
Fort Atkinson, Wisconsin 53538
Contact: Director
Ph: (920) 563-7769
Fax: (920) 568-3203
E-mail: info@hoardmuseum.org
Web: www.hoardmuseum.org

Institutional, Public
Size: 60
Date Range: 19th–20th
Lend: Yes
Copy: Yes

Details: Sunday school songbooks, some in German and Scandinavian languages, dating from 1850–1930.

Denominations: *Lutheran*

325. University of Wisconsin at Madison [1988]
Mills Music Library
B162 Memorial Library
728 State St.
Madison, Wisconsin 53706
Contact: Director
Ph: (608) 263-1884

Institutional, Public
Size: 260
Date Range: 17th–20th

Fax: (608) 265-2754
E-mail: askmusic@library.wisc.edu
Web: www.library.wisc.edu/libraries/Music

Details: About 260 partly cataloged hymnals. Uncataloged are gospel songbooks, Sunday school songbooks, and general hymnals ca. 1900. Hymnals dating from 1676, in twenty-two languages.

Denominations: *Anglican, Buddhist, Catholic, Christian Science, Episcopal, Evangelical and Reformed, Hindu, Lutheran, Methodist, Moravian, Presbyterian, Shaker, Unitarian, United Church of Christ*

326. First Presbyterian Church [1988]
Institutional, Private
Size: 80
406 Grant St.
Wausau, Wisconsin 54403
Contact: Librarian
Ph: (715) 842-2116
Web: www.firstpreswausau.org

Details: About eighty partly cataloged hymnals and volumes on hymnology, including a words-only edition of *Gospel Hymns Consolidated* (nos. 1–4). Emphasis on youth hymnals from the 1920s.

Bibliography

This bibliography is divided into four sections: Studies of Hymnals by Denomination, Studies of Hymnals across Denominations, Descriptions of Hymnal Collections, and Reference Works in Hymnology.

STUDIES OF HYMNALS BY DENOMINATION

Amish

Bartel, Lee. "The Tradition of the Amish in Music." *The Hymn* 37, no. 4 (October 1986): 20–26.

Hessler, Martin. "Hymnbooks Used by the Old Order Amish." *The Hymn* 28, no. 1 (January 1977): 11–16.

Anglican (*see also* Episcopal)

Ellinwood, Leonard. "*Hymns Ancient and Modern* in America." *The Hymn* 12, no. 4 (October 1961): 107–112.

Millman, Thomas. "An Early Canadian Psalm Book." *Journal of the Canadian Church Historical Society* 29 (April 1987): 32–34.

Wilson, John. "Hymns for Today and Tomorrow." *English Church Music* (1972): 36–50.

Note: these citations refer to usage of Anglican works in North America. There is a wide range of literature on Anglican hymnals beyond what is listed here.

Apostolic Christian Church of America

Klopfenstein, Perry A. *A Treasure of Praise: A History of the* Zion's Harp Hymnal. 3rd ed. Gridley, Ill.: Klopfenstein, 1984.

Baptist

Archer, J. Douglas. "A Comparison of Hymnals: [Church of the Brethren, Mennonite, Baptist, Disciples, Methodist]." *Brethren Life and Thought* 33 (autumn 1988): 265–269.

Brewster, C. Ray. "Jesse Mercer's *Cluster*." *Viewpoints: Georgia Baptist History* 8 (1982): 33–49.

Coffman, Sue. "In the Beginning Were the Words: But Not the Same Yesterday, Today, and Forever: Textual Changes in Three Recent Hymnals [language issues in UMC, PCUSA and SBC hymnals]." *The Hymn* 44, no. 2 (April 1993): 6–11.

Eskew, Harry. "Southern Baptist Contributions to Hymnody." *Baptist Hymnody and Heritage* 19, no. 1 (January 1984): 27–35.

———. "Use and Influence of Hymnals in Southern Baptist Churches up to 1915." *Baptist History and Heritage* 21, no. 3 (1986): 21–30.

Gregory, David Louis. "Southern Baptist Hymnals (1956, 1975, 1991) as Sourcebooks for Worship in Southern Baptist Churches." D.M.A. diss., Southern Baptist Theological Seminary, 1994.

Hedger, Wayne L. *Baptist Hymnal Indices: Considering the 1991* Baptist Hymnal, *1975* Baptist Hymnal, *1956* Baptist Hymnal, *and 1940* Broadman Hymnal. Cleveland, Tenn.: Glory, 1993.

McDuffie, Dennis Vernon. "The *Baptist Hymnal,* 1883: A Centennial Study." Master's thesis, Southern Baptist Theological Seminary, 1983.

McElrath, Hugh T. "Turning Points in the Story of Baptist Church Music." *Baptist History and Heritage* 19, no. 1 (1984): 4–16.

Murrell, Irvin Henry. "An Examination of Southern Antebellum Baptist Hymnals and Tunebooks as Indicators of the Congregational Hymn and Tune Repertories of the Period with an Analysis of Representative Tunes." D.M.A. diss., New Orleans Baptist Theological Seminary, 1984.

Music, David W. "Baptist Hymnals as Shapers of Worship." *Baptist History and Heritage* 31, no. 3 (1996): 7–17.

———. "The First American Baptist Tunebook." *Foundations* 23, no. 3 (1980): 267–273.

———. "J. R. Graves' *The Little Seraph* (1874): A Memphis Tunebook." *West Tennessee Historical Society Papers* 35 (1981): 40–50.

Reynolds, William J. "Our Heritage of Baptist Hymnody in America." *Baptist History and Heritage* 11, no. 4 (1976): 204–217.

Richardson, Paul A. "Sweet Chants that Led My Steps Abroad: Anglican Chant in Nineteenth-Century American Baptist Hymnals." In

We'll Shout and Sing Hosanna, edited by David W. Music and William Jensen Reynolds, 155–184. Fort Worth, Tex.: Southwestern Baptist Theological Seminary, 1998.

Rose, Richard Wayne. "*The Psalmist:* A Significant Hymnal for Baptists in America during the Nineteenth Century." D.M.A. diss., Southwestern Baptist Theological Seminary, 1991.

Simoneaux, Michel. "An Evaluation of the *Baptist Hymnal* (1956) in Comparison with Five Hymnals Previously Popular among Southern Baptists from 1904 until 1956." Ed.D. diss., New Orleans Baptist Theological Seminary, 1969.

Singer, David. "God and Man in Baptist Hymnals, 1784–1844." *Mid-Continent American Studies Journal* 9, no. 2 (1968): 14–26.

Spencer, Jon Michael. "The Hymnody of the National Baptist Convention." *The Hymn* 41, no. 2 (April 1990): 7–18.

Brethren

Archer, J. Douglas. "A Comparison of Hymnals: [Church of the Brethren, Mennonite, Baptist, Disciples, Methodist]." *Brethren Life and Thought* 33 (autumn 1988): 265–269.

Beery, William. *Brethren Hymns, Hymnals, Authors, and Composers: A Study in Our Literary and Musical Heritage*. Elgin, Ill.: Board of Christian Education, Church of the Brethren, 1929.

Durnbaugh, Hedwig T. "*Geistreiches Gesang-Buch,* 1720: The First Brethren Hymnal." *The Hymn* 42, no. 4 (October 1991): 20–23.

———. *The German Hymnody of the Brethren, 1720–1903*. Brethren Encyclopedia Monograph Series, no. 1. Philadelphia: Brethren Encyclopedia, 1986.

Faus, Nancy Rosenberger, ed. *The Importance of Music in Worship*. Elgin, Ill.: Brethren Press, 1993.

Hinks, Donald R. *Brethren Hymn Books and Hymnals, 1720–1884*. Gettysburg, Penn.: Brethren Heritage Press, 1986.

Porter, Ellen J. "American Folk Hymns in Three Nineteenth-Century United Brethren Hymnals." *The Hymn* 48, no. 1 (January 1997): 28–29.

Catholic

Banovitz, Dawn Helen. "The Development of the Canadian National Catholic Hymnal: *Catholic Book of Worship* (1972), *Catholic Book of Worship II* (1980), and *Catholic Book of Worship III* (1994)." Ph.D. diss., University of Iowa, 1994.

Boccardi, Donald. *The History of American Catholic Hymnals since Vatican II*. Chicago: GIA Publications, 2001.

Finn, Peter C. "Bibliography of Hymnals in Use in American and Canadian Roman Catholic Churches." *The Hymn* 29, no. 2 (April 1978): 98–100+.

Gasslein, Bernadette. "*Catholic Book of Worship III* as an Agent of Ecumenism." *Ecumenism* 122 (June 1996): 24–27.

Grimes, Robert R. "John Aitken and Catholic Music in Federal Philadelphia." *American Music* 16, no. 3 (fall 1998): 289–310.

Gumula, Stanislaus. "Mepkin Abbey's Homemade Hymnals." *The Hymn* 34, no. 2 (April 1983): 100–101.

Haban, Teresine. "The Hymnody of the Roman Catholic Church: Historical Survey with an Analysis of Musical Styles." Ph.D. diss., University of Rochester, 1956.

Higginson, J. Vincent. "Catholic Hymnals and Psalter Melodies." *The Hymn* 17, no. 2 (April 1966): 42–44+.

———. *History of American Catholic Hymnals: Survey and Background*. [Springfield, Ohio]: Hymn Society of America, 1982.

Katra, William. "A Mexican Hymnal and the Struggle for Justice." *Theology Today* 43, no. 4 (January 1987): 524–532.

Leaver, Robin. "Three Hymnals: Different Denominational Emphasis but One Song?" *Worship* 61 (January 1987): 45–60.

Monkres, Lynn Hugh. "The *Saint Gregory Hymnal and Catholic Choir Book:* Analysis and Hymnal Companion." Ph.D. diss., Catholic University of America, 1991.

Piscitelli, Felicia A. "Thirty-Five Years of Catholic Hymnals in the United States (1962–1997): A Chronological Listing." *The Hymn* 49, no. 4 (October 1998): 21–34.

Routley, Erik. "Contemporary Catholic Hymnody: An Afterword." *Worship* 47 (August–September 1973): 417–423.

———. "The Larger Hymnals: [Contemporary Catholic Hymnody in Its Wider Setting, Pt. 1]." *Worship* 47 (April 1973): 194–211.

———. "The Smaller Hymnals: [Contemporary Catholic Hymnody in Its Wider Setting, Pt. 2]." *Worship* 47 (May 1973): 258–273.

Smith, William Farley. "*Lead Me, Guide Me: The African American Catholic Hymnal*." *The Hymn* 40, no. 1 (January 1989): 13–15.

Verret, Mary Camilla. *A Preliminary Survey of Roman Catholic Hymnals Published in the United States of America*. Master's thesis, Catholic University of America, 1964.

Watson, Wendelin J. "*Lead Me, Guide Me: The African American Catholic Hymnal*." *Journal of Black Sacred Music* 3 (spring 1989): 68–71.

Wilson, John. "Hymns for Today and Tomorrow." *English Church Music* (1972): 36–50.

Christadelphian

Roberts, Maynard Wesley. "The Hymnody of Christadelphians: A Survey of Hymnists and Hymn Collections." *The Hymn* 48, no. 3 (July 1997): 44–51.

Christian and Missionary Alliance

Rivard, Eugene. "The Hymnody of the Christian and Missionary Alliance (1891–1978) as a Reflection of Its Theology and Development." D.M.A. diss., Southwestern Baptist Theological Seminary, 1991.

Christian Church (Disciples of Christ)

Archer, J. Douglas. "A Comparison of Hymnals: [Church of the Brethren, Mennonite, Baptist, Disciples, Methodist]." *Brethren Life and Thought* 33 (autumn 1988): 265–269.

Barclay, Earle. "Hymnody of the Christian Church." *The American Organist* 14 (September 1980): 23.

Dowling, Enos. "The Alexander Campbell Hymn Book (1828–1865)." *Restoration Quarterly* 30, nos. 2–3 (1988): 145–158.

———. *Hymn and Gospel Song Books of the Restoration Movement: A Preliminary Bibliography*. 2nd ed. Lincoln, Ill.: Jessie C. Eury Library, Lincoln Christian College and Seminary, 1988.

———. *Hymn Books of the Christian Church or Christian Connexion Sometimes Called "Newlights": A Preliminary Bibliography*. Lincoln, Ill.: Lincoln Christian College, 1984.

———, comp. *Of Men and Psalmody and Hymn Books*. N.p.: n.p., 1989.

Hanson, K. C. "The Hymnology and Hymnals of the Restoration Movement." B.Div. thesis, Butler University, 1951.

Merrick, Daniel B. "Sing to the Lord: Hymnology among the Disciples." *Mid-Stream* 36, no. 3/4 (1997): 309–318.

Morgan, Peter M. "Disciples Hymnbooks: A Continuing Quest for Harmony." *Discipliana* 55 (summer 1995): 46–63.

Teague, Kenneth Pat. "A Study of the Development of Hymnals in the Restoration Movement." Master's thesis, Harding College Graduate School of Bible and Religion, 1959.

Turner, Nancy M. "The *Chalice Hymnal:* Broken Bread–One Body." *The Hymn* 48, no. 1 (January 1997): 33–38.

Church of God

Adams, Robert Alvin. "The Hymnody of the Church of God (1885–1980) as a Reflection of That Church's Theological and Cultural Changes." Ph.D. diss., Southwestern Baptist Theological Seminary, 1980.

Spencer, Jon Michael. "Yes, Lord: the Church of God in Christ Hymnal." *Journal of Black Sacred Music* 1 (spring 1987): 53–60.

Church of Jesus Christ of Latter-day Saints

Briggs, Robert Keith. "The 1844 Bellows Falls Hymnal: Its Significance in Early Latter-day Saint Hymnody and an Historical Survey of Its Sources." D.A. diss., University of Northern Colorado, 1995.

Campbell, Douglas. "Changes in LDS Hymns: Implications and Opportunities." *Dialogue* 28 (fall 1995): 65–91.

Jacobs, L. R. *Mormon Non-English Scriptures, Hymnals, and Periodicals, 1830–1986: A Descriptive Bibliography, with Appendices Which List All Other Publications by Mormon Authors in Danish and Swedish from 1839 to ca. 1900*. Salt Lake City, Utah: n.p., 1991.

Poulter, Mary. "Doctrines of Faith and Hope Found in Emma Smith's 1835 Hymnbook." *BYU Studies* 37, no. 2 (1997–1998): 32–56.

———. "The First Ten Years of Latter-day Saint Hymnody: A Study of Emma Smith's 1835 and Little and Gardner's 1844 Hymnals." Master's thesis, University of Massachusetts, 1995.

Wilkes, William Leroy, Jr. "Borrowed Music in Mormon Hymnals." Ph.D. diss., University of Southern California, 1957.

Churches of Christ

Bowman, John. *Sweetly the Tones Are Falling: A Hymnal History of Churches of Christ*. Brentwood, Tenn.: Penmann Press, 1984.

Dowling, Enos, comp. *Of Men and Psalmody and Hymn Books*. N.p.: n.p., 1989.

Holland, Harold E. "The Hymnody of the Churches of Christ." *The Hymn* 30, no. 4 (October 1979): 263–268.

Shepard, Dane K. "An Analysis of Three Hymnals Used by the Churches of Christ." Master's thesis, California State University, Fullerton, 1980.

Community of Christ

Lynn, Karen. "The 1981 RLDS Hymnal: Songs More Brightly Sung." *Dialogue* 16, no. 4 (1983): 33–41.

Disciples of Christ (*see* Christian Church (Disciples of Christ))

Ephrata Cloister

Bach, Jeffery Alan. "Voices of the Turtledoves: The Mystical Language of the Ephrata Cloister." Ph.D. diss., Duke University, 1997.

Duck, Dorothy Hampton. "The Art and Artists of the Ephrata Cloister." *Journal of the Lancaster County Historical Society* 97, no. 4 (1995): 134–151.

Main, Kari M. "Illuminated Hymnals of the Ephrata Cloister." *Winterthur Portfolio* 32, no. 1 (1997): 65–78.

Episcopal (*see also* Anglican)

Albritton, Sherrodd. "What's Going on with the Hymnal?" *Historical Magazine of the Protestant Episcopal Church* 48 (June 1979): 133–144.

Eskew, Harry. "Returning to Our Musical Roots: Early Shape-Note Tunes in Recent American Hymnals." In *With Ever Joyful Hearts: Essays on Liturgy and Music Honoring Marion J. Hatchett,* edited by J. Neil Alexander, 261–271. New York: Church Publishing Incorporated, 1999.

Gable, Martin Dewey, Jr. "The Hymnody of the Church, 1789–1832." *Historical Magazine of the Protestant Episcopal Church* 36, no. 3 (1967): 249–270.

Glover, Raymond F. "Erik Routley and the Episcopal *Hymnal 1982.*" In *Duty and Delight: Routley Remembered,* edited by Robin A. Leaver and others, 153–158. Carol Stream, Ill.: Hope Publishing Company, 1985.

———. "Theology in Song: The Hymnody of the Episcopal Church." In *A New Conversation: Essays on the Future of Theology and the Episcopal Church,* edited by Robert Boak Slocum, 297–305. New York: Church Publishing, 1999.

Leaver, Robin. "Three Hymnals: Different Denominational Emphasis but One Song?" *Worship* 61 (January 1987): 45–60.

Ogasapian, John. "Some Notes on the Episcopal *Hymnal 1982*." *Journal of Church Music* 29 (November 30, 1987): 4–7+.

Parker, Olean. "American Protestant Hymnody as Reflected in Contemporary Methodist and Episcopalian Hymnals." B.A. thesis, [West Liberty State College], 1984.

Schalk, Carl. "Sounding in Glad Adoration: Critical Impressions of *The Hymnal 1982*." *The Hymn* 38, no. 2 (April 1987): 17–20.

Spencer, Jon Michael. "'Lord, Dear Lord Above': The Development and Content of *Lift Every Voice and Sing* Hymnbook." *Anglican and Episcopal History* 59, no. 2 (1990): 243–257.

Evangelical Covenant Church of America

Durnbaugh, Hedda. "*The Covenant Hymnal,* 1973: First Lines of Nordic Hymntexts in Translation." *The Hymn* 40, no. 1 (January 1989): 29–32.

Erickson, J. Irving. "Covenant Hymnody and the Covenant Hymnal of 1973." *Covenant Quarterly* 31 (November 1973): 12–22.

Lindquist, Edwin P. "The Hymnody of the Evangelical Covenant Church: Its First One Hundred Years." Master's thesis, California State University, Hayward, 1986.

Friends (Quaker)

Music, David W. "*Worship in Song: A Friends Hymnal*." *The Hymn* 49 (July 1998): 35–38.

Hutterite

Lieseberg, Ursula. "The Martyr Songs of the Hutterite Brethren." *Mennonite Quarterly Review* 67 (July 1993): 323–337.

Judaic

Schiller, Benjie-Ellen. "The Hymnal as an Index of Musical Change in Reform Synagogues." In *Sacred Sound and Social Change: Liturgical Music in Jewish and Christian Experience,* edited by Lawrence A. Hoffman and Janet R. Walton, 187–213. Notre Dame, Ind.: University of Notre Dame Press, 1992.

Lutheran

Anderson, Verlyn Dean. "The History and Acculturation of the English Language Hymnals of the Norwegian-American Lutheran Churches, 1879–1958." Ph.D. diss., University of Minnesota, 1972.

Archie, Victor Robert. *An Analysis of the Symbolism in the Words and Music of the Hymns Pertaining to the Resurrection of Our Lord as Published in the Common Service Hymnal of the United Lutheran Church of America*. Master's thesis, Northwestern University, 1956.

Brauer, James Leonard. "The Hymnals of the Lutheran Church–Missouri Synod." Master's thesis, Concordia Seminary, 1967.

Brown, Edgar S., Jr. "First Person Singular: The *Lutheran Book of Worship:* Where Do We Go from Here?" In "Studying the Lutheran Book of Worship," edited by Carl Schalk. *Church Music* 79 (1979): 92–96.

Cartford, Gerhard M. "Music for Youth in an Emerging Church." *Norwegian-American Studies* 22 (1965): 162–177.

Doan, Gilbert E. Jr. "Consensus and Compromise: Some Political Perspectives on the *Lutheran Book of Worship*." In "Studying the Lutheran Book of Worship," edited by Carl Schalk. *Church Music* 79 (1979): 55–59.

Eskew, Harry. "The *Lutheran Book of Worship*: One Baptist's Reaction." In "Studying the Lutheran Book of Worship," edited by Carl Schalk. *Church Music* 79 (1979): 85–86.

Fuchs, John M. "From *The Lutheran Hymnal* to *Lutheran Worship:* A Paradigm of Lutheran Church–Missouri Synod History." *Concordia Journal* 20 (April 1994): 130–146.

Gilbert, Dan Paul. "How the Missouri Synod Accepted the *Lutheran Hymnal* of 1941." *Concordia Historical Institute Quarterly* 51, no. 1 (1978): 23–27.

Green, Lowell C. "The Chorales of Martin Luther: How Have They Fared in the *Lutheran Book of Worship*." In "Studying the Lutheran Book of Worship," edited by Carl Schalk. *Church Music* 79 (1979): 60–65.

Grime, Paul J., D. Richard Stuckwisch, and Jon D. Vieker, eds. *Through the Church the Song Goes on: Preparing a Lutheran Hymnal for the Twenty-First Century*. St. Louis: Commission on Worship, the Lutheran Church–Missouri Synod, 1999.

Grimminger, Daniel Jay. "*Das Neu Eingerichtete Gesangbuch* of 1821: A Forgotten Voice of Ohio Lutheranism." *The Hymn* 52, no. 1 (January 2001): 7–15.

Grindal, Gracia. "Dano-Norwegian Hymnody in America." *Lutheran Quarterly* 6, no. 3 (1992): 257–315.

"An Interview with Eugene Brand: Project Director for the *Lutheran Book of Worship*." In "Studying the Lutheran Book of Worship," edited by Carl Schalk. *Church Music* 79 (1979): 67–69.

"An Interview with Richard Hillert: Music Editor for the *Lutheran Book of Worship*." In "Studying the Lutheran Book of Worship," edited by Carl Schalk. *Church Music* 79 (1979): 70–76.

Janzow, Samuel. "Some Thoughts on Translating Luther's Hymns into English." In "Studying the Lutheran Book of Worship," edited by Carl Schalk. *Church Music* 79 (1979): 66.

Kosche, Kenneth. *Luther's Hymns in Lutheran Hymnals of the United States: A Brief Survey*. Mequon, Wis.: Concordia College, 1986.

Laetsch, Leonard. "Aspects of Worship Practices in the History of the Lutheran Church–Missouri Synod." *Concordia Historical Institute Quarterly* 70, no. 4 (winter 1997): 147–163.

Litton, James. "An Episcopalian Looks at the *Lutheran Book of Worship*." In "Studying the Lutheran Book of Worship," edited by Carl Schalk. *Church Music* 79 (1979): 90–91.

Nordin, John P. "'They've Changed the Hymns': or, An Investigation of Changes in Hymnody in the Hymnbooks of the Evangelical Lutheran Church in America." *The Hymn* 47, no. 1 (January 1996): 25–33.

Pannebaker, Jeffrey Roy. "Early Lutheran Music in America: The Hymnody of the General Synod." Ph.D. diss., University of Pittsburgh, 1998.

Pirner, Reuben G. "The Hymns of the *Lutheran Book of Worship* as Cultural Modes." In "Studying the Lutheran Book of Worship," edited by Carl Schalk. *Church Music* 79 (1979): 81–84.

Precht, Fred L., ed. *Lutheran Worship: History and Practice*. St. Louis: Concordia Publishing House, 1993.

Rusert, Matthew L. "Do the Three LCMS Hymnals Follow the Lutheran Confessions in Their Common Hymn Texts Describing the Lord's Supper?" Master's thesis, Concordia Theological Seminary, 1985.

Schalk, Carl. *God's Song in a New Land: Lutheran Hymnals in America*. Concordia Scholarship Today. St. Louis: Concordia, 1995.

———. *The Roots of Hymnody in the Lutheran Church, Missouri Synod: The Story of Congregational Song, the Hymnals and the Chorale Books from the Saxon Immigration to the Present*. Church Music Pamphlet Series, Hymnology, no. 2. St. Louis: Concordia Publishing House, 1965.

———, ed. "Studying the *Lutheran Book of Worship*." *Church Music* 79 (1979): 54–96.

Sensmeier, Randall K. "The Influence of the Worship Supplement on the *Lutheran Book of Worship*." In "Studying the Lutheran Book of Worship," edited by Carl Schalk. *Church Music* 79 (1979): 77–80.

Vieker, Jon D. "C. F. W. Walther, Editor of Missouri's First and Only German Hymnal." *Concordia Historical Institute Quarterly* 65, no. 2 (1992): 53–69.

Westermeyer, Paul. "Lineaments of the Reformed and Lutheran Traditions: Liturgy and Hymnody in Nineteenth-Century Pennsylvania." *Church Music* 80 (1980): 2–22.

Wolf, Edward C. "America's First Lutheran Chorale Book: [with Foreword and Introduction to 1813 Hymnal]." *Concordia Historical Institute Quarterly* 46 (spring 1973): 5–17.

———. "Lutheran Hymnody and Music Published in America 1700–1850: A Descriptive Bibliography." *Concordia Historical Institute Quarterly* 50 (1977): 164–185.

———. *Peter Erben and America's First Lutheran Tunebook in English*. New York: Garland, 1994.

Young, Carlton R. "The *Southern Harmony* and the *Lutheran Book of Worship*." In "Studying the Lutheran Book of Worship," edited by Carl Schalk. *Church Music* 79 (1979): 87–88.

Mennonite

Archer, J. Douglas. "A Comparison of Hymnals: [Church of the Brethren, Mennonite, Baptist, Disciples, Methodist]." *Brethren Life and Thought* 33 (autumn 1988): 265–269.

Bender, Harold S. "The Hymnology of the Anabaptists." *The Mennonite Quarterly Review* 31, no. 1 (January 1957): 5–10.

Berg, W. "The Music of the Mennonite Brethren of Saskatchewan to 1923." *American Music* 4, no. 4 (1986): 457–468.

Faus, Nancy Rosenberger, ed. *The Importance of Music in Worship*. Elgin, Ill.: Brethren Press, 1993.

Gross, Suzanne E. "Hymnody of Easter Pennsylvania German Mennonite Communities: Notenbüchlein (Manuscript Songbooks) from 1780 to 1835." Ph.D. diss., University of Maryland, 1994.

Hiebert, Clarence. "The Making of a New Mennonite Brethren Hymnal." *Direction* 22, no. 2 (fall 1993): 60–71.

Horch, Benjamin. "A Mennonite Hymnal for Canada." *The Hymn* 12, no. 3 (July 1961): 93–95.

Hostetler, James C. *The Mennonite Hymnal in America since 1742*. N.p.: n.p., 1950.

Oyer, Mary. *Exploring the Mennonite Hymnal: Essays*. Worship Series 7a. Newton, Kans.: Faith and Life, 1980.

———. *Exploring the Mennonite Hymnal: Handbook*. Worship Series 7b. Newton, Kans.: Faith and Life, 1983.

Ressler, Martin E. *An Annotated Bibliography of Mennonite Hymnals and Songbooks, 1742–1986*. Quarryville, Pa.: A. Ressler; Lancaster, Pa.: Lancaster Mennonite Historical Society, 1987.

———. "*Ein Unpartheyisches Gesang-Buch*." *Pennsylvania Mennonite Heritage* 2, no. 4 (1979): 13–19.

Smucker, David Rempel. "Singing God's Praise in Two Nations and Two Tongues: A Comparison of Two Mennonite Hymnals and Their Preparation." *Mennonite Quarterly Review* 73, no. 3 (1999): 615–630.

Stolzfus, Philip E. "Tradition and Diversity in *Ein Unpartheyisches Gesangbuch*." *Pennsylvania Mennonite Heritage* 17, no. 2 (1994): 29–36.

Methodist

Adell, Marian Y. "The 'Body of Christ' in Methodist Hymnody: Dis-remembered and Remembered." In *Proceedings of the North American Academy of Liturgy*. Valparaiso, Ind.: The Academy, 1996.

Anderson, Fred R. "Three New Voices: Singing God's Song [Christian Reformed Psalter Hymnal; United Methodist Hymnal; Presbyterian Hymnal]." *Theology Today* 47 (October 1990): 260–272.

Archer, J. Douglas. "A Comparison of Hymnals: [Church of the Brethren, Mennonite, Baptist, Disciples, Methodist]." *Brethren Life and Thought* 33 (autumn 1988): 265–269.

Baldridge, Terry L. "Evolving Tastes in Hymntunes of the Methodist Episcopal Church in the Nineteenth Century." Ph.D. diss., University of Kansas, 1982.

Bray, Carolyn Sue Kolby. "The United Methodist Hymnal: Entering the Third Century." D.Min. diss., Wesley Theological Seminary, 1990.

Coffman, Sue. "In the Beginning Were the Words: But Not the Same Yesterday, Today, and Forever: Textual Changes in Three Recent Hymnals [language issues in UMC, PCUSA, and SBC hymnals]." *The Hymn* 44, no. 2 (April 1993): 6–11.

Cook, Roland. "Changing Theological Expression as Reflected in the Successive Editions of the Methodist Hymnal." Master's thesis, Drew University, 1949.

Divers, Jessyca Pauline. "The African Methodist Episcopal Church and Its Hymnal." Master's thesis, Northwestern University, 1974.

Doran, Carol, and Thomas H. Troeger. "The United Methodist Hymnal." *Worship* 65 (March 1991): 159–169.

Flathers, Judy Marlene. "An Analytical Study of Contemporary Christian Music in *The Hymnal for Worship and Celebration* (Word Music, 1986)." Master's thesis, Seattle Pacific University, 1988.

Gallaway, Craig. "Patterns of Worship in Early Methodist Hymnody, and the Task of Hymnal Revision." *Quarterly Review* 7 (fall 1987): 14–29.

———. "Tradition Meets Revision: The Impact of the Wesley Hymn Corpus on the New *United Methodist Hymnal*." *Quarterly Review* 9 (fall 1989): 64–79.

Graham, Fred Kimball. "'With One Heart and One Voice': A Core Repertory of Hymn Tunes Published for Use in the Methodist Episcopal Church in the United States, 1808–1878." Ph.D. diss., Drew University, 1991.

Harmon, Nolan B. "Creating Official Methodist Hymnals." *Methodist History* 16, no. 4 (1978): 230–244.

———. "Recalling the Human Side of Revising Our Hymnals." *The Hymn* 24, no. 3 (July 1973): 77–80.

Heisey, Terry. "Singet Hallelujah." *Methodist History* 28 (July 1990): 237–251.

Hicks, Roger Wayne. "The First Southern Methodist Hymn Book." *The Hymn* 48, no. 4 (October 1997): 32–35.

Hum, Stephen. "'When We Were No People, Then We Were A People': Evangelical Language and the Free Blacks of Philadelphia in the Early Republic [First hymnal of the AME Church of Philadelphia, 1801–1818]." In *A Mighty Baptism,* edited by Susan Juster and Lisa MacFarlane, 235–258. Ithaca, N.Y.: Cornell University Press, 1996.

Mora Martinez, Raquel. "*Mil Voces Para Celebrar: Himnario Metodista*." *The Hymn* 49, no. 2 (April 1998): 25–29.

Parker, Olean. "American Protestant Hymnody as Reflected in Contemporary Methodist and Episcopalian Hymnals." B.A. thesis, [West Liberty State College], 1984.

Porter, Ellen Jane Lorenz. "The Hymnody of the Evangelical United Brethren Church." *Journal of Theology* (United Theological Seminary) 91 (1987): 74–81.

———. "*The Revivalist.*" *The Hymn* 41, no. 2 (April 1990): 26–29.

Price, Carl Fowler. *Curiosities of the Hymnal.* New York: The Methodist Book Concern, 1926.

———. *The Music and Hymnody of the Methodist Hymnal.* New York: The Methodist Book Concern, 1926.

Rehwalt, Peter W. "Splashing in the Ever-Rolling Stream: The Arts at Work in *The United Methodist Hymnal* and *The New Century Hymnal.*" *The Hymn* 52, no. 4 (October 2001): 19–29.

Riel, Jennifer. "Voices in Harmony: Methodist and Presbyterian Hymn Books prior to Church Union." *Touchstone* 15, no. 1 (January 1997): 38–44.

Rogal, Samuel J., comp. *Guide to the Hymns and Tunes of American Methodism.* Music Reference Collection, no. 7. New York: Greenwood Press, 1986.

Rowe, Kenneth E. "The 1989 United Methodist Hymnal in Historical Perspective." *Drew Gateway* 60 (fall 1990): 74–78.

Scott, Carol. "Common Foundations: The Hymnals of the United Methodist Church and the Black Methodist Denominations." Master's thesis, Associated Mennonite Biblical Seminary, 1999.

Sheaffer, Aaron Milton. *The Historical Evolution of the Hymnal in the Evangelical United Brethren Church.* N.p.: n.p., 1958.

Spencer, Jon Michael. "The Hymnal of the Christian Methodist Episcopal Church." *Journal of Black Sacred Music* 3 (spring 1989): 53–67.

———. "The Hymnody of the African Methodist Episcopal Church." *American Music* 8, no. 3 (fall 1990): 274–293.

Stevenson, George J. *The Methodist Hymn-Book and Its Associations.* 2nd ed. London: Hamilton, Adams, 1872.

Strauss, Barbara J. "The Methodist/Moravian Legacy of Hymns." *Methodist History* 24, no. 3 (April 1986): 179–190.

Volland, Linda L. "Three Centuries of Methodist Hymnody: An Historical Overview of the Development of the American Methodist Hymnal with Special Attention to Hymnody in the 1780, 1878, and 1989 Hymnals." D.M.A. diss., University of Nebraska, 1995.

Yardley, Anne Bagnall. "What besides Hymns? The Tune Books of Early Methodism." *Methodist History* 37, no. 3 (1999): 189–201.

Moravian

Adams, Charles B. "Moravians Produce a New Hymnal." *The Hymn* 20, no. 4 (October 1969): 101–107.

———. *Our Moravian Hymn Heritage: Chronological Listing of Hymns and Tunes of Moravian Origin in the American Moravian Hymnal of 1969*. [Bethlehem, Pa.]: Dept. of Publications, Moravian Church in America, 1984.

Arndal, Steffen. "Awakening and Singing in German Pietism and Moravianism." Translated by Hedda Durnbaugh. *The Hymn* 36, no. 3 (July 1985): 11–14.

———. "Spiritual Revival and Hymnody: The Hymnbooks of German Pietism and Moravianism." Edited and translated by Hedwig T. Durnbaugh. *Brethren Life and Thought* 40, no. 2 (1995): 70–93.

Johanson, John Henry. "Moravian Hymnody." *The Hymn* 30, no. 3 (July 1979): 167–177+; no. 4 (October 1979): 230–239+.

Strauss, Barbara J. "The Methodist/Moravian Legacy of Hymns." *Methodist History* 24, no. 3 (April 1986): 179–190.

Williams, Henry Llewellyn. *The Development of the Moravian Hymnal*. N.p.: n.p., 1962.

Nondenominational

Booth, John David. "A Comparative Study of Four Major Nondenominational, Evangelical, American Hymnals in Current Use." D.M.A. diss., New Orleans Baptist Theological Seminary, 1986.

Orthodox

Brearley, Denis G. *The Publishing of the Russian Orthodox Church Music, 1700 to the Present*. Kanata, Ontario: D. Brearley, 1997.

Pentecostal

Johnson, Robert A. "A Bibliography of Hymnals Published by American Pentecostal Denominations." *The Hymn* 38, no. 1 (January 1987): 29–30.

Spencer, Jon Michael. "The Heavenly Anthem: Holy Ghost Singing in the Primal Pentecostal Revival (1906–1909)." *Journal of Black Sacred Music* 1, no. 1 (spring 1987): 1–33.

Presbyterian

Anderson, Fred R. "Three New Voices: Singing God's Song [Christian Reformed Psalter Hymnal; United Methodist Hymnal; Presbyterian Hymnal]." *Theology Today* 47 (October 1990): 260–272.

Bower, Peter C., ed. "The Presbyterian Hymnal." *Reformed Liturgy and Music* 24 (spring 1990): 53–90, 99–107.

Coffman, Sue. "In the Beginning Were the Words: But Not the Same Yesterday, Today, and Forever: Textual Changes in Three Recent Hymnals [language issues in UMC, PCUSA, and SBC hymnals]." *The Hymn* 44, no. 2 (April 1993): 6–11.

Cooper, G. Kenneth. "Time to Renew Congregational Singing." In "The Presbyterian Hymnal," edited by Peter C. Bower. *Reformed Liturgy and Music* 24 (spring 1990): 100.

Costen, Melva W. "Why This New Hymnal." In "The Presbyterian Hymnal," edited by Peter C. Bower. *Reformed Liturgy and Music* 24 (spring 1990): 60–62.

Ehrhardt, Charles R. "Problems and Challenges Facing the Hymnbook Committee." In "The Presbyterian Hymnal," edited by Peter C. Bower. *Reformed Liturgy and Music* 24 (spring 1990): 63–65.

Hicks, Roger Wayne. "Louis F. Benson's 1895 Presbyterian Hymnal Innovation." *The Hymn* 47, no. 2 (April 1996): 17–21.

Hymnody of the Presbyterian Church. Philadelphia: Hymnal Division Publications Dept., Presbyterian Board of Christian Education, 1930.

Kadel, Richard William. "The Evolution of Hymnody in the Presbyterian Church in the United States, 1850–1900." Master's thesis, Florida State University, 1968.

Kerr, Hugh T. "The 1906 Book of Common Worship: An Amusing Footnote." *Journal of Presbyterian History* 58 (summer 1980): 182–184.

Leaver, Robin A. "The Hymnbook as a Book of Practical Theology." In "The Presbyterian Hymnal," edited by Peter C. Bower. *Reformed Liturgy and Music* 24 (spring 1990): 55–57.

Loh, I-To. "Contributions of 'Asian' Traditions to the Hymnal." In "The Presbyterian Hymnal," edited by Peter C. Bower. *Reformed Liturgy and Music* 24 (spring 1990): 80–81.

Lovelace, Austin. "*The Hymnal,* by Louis F. Benson." *American Presbyterians* 66, no. 4 (1988): 288–293.

McKim, LindaJo. "The Ordering of a Hymnal." In "The Presbyterian Hymnal," edited by Peter C. Bower. *Reformed Liturgy and Music* 24 (spring 1990): 77–79.

Morrison, Rheta Hope. "A Correlated Use of the Graded Hymnals in the Presbyterian Church in the U.S.A." Master's thesis, San Francisco Theological Seminary, 1951.

Partington, David C. "Psalms in the Presbyterian Hymnal: Making Them User-Friendly." In "The Presbyterian Hymnal," edited by Peter C. Bower. *Reformed Liturgy and Music* 24 (spring 1990): 72–74.

Powell, Paul Richard. "Louis F. Benson, the 1895 Presbyterian Hymnal, and Twentieth-Century American Hymnody." Ph.D. diss., Drew University, 1998.

Riel, Jennifer. "Voices in Harmony: Methodist and Presbyterian Hymn Books prior to Church Union." *Touchstone* 15, no. 1 (January 1997): 38–44.

Rodriguez, Jose A. "Hispanic Hymns in the New Hymnal." In "The Presbyterian Hymnal," edited by Peter C. Bower. *Reformed Liturgy and Music* 24 (spring 1990): 82–83.

Simmons, Morgan F. "Hymnody: Its Place in Twentieth-Century Presbyterianism." In *Confessional Mosaic: Presbyterians and Twentieth-Century Theology,* edited by Milton J. Coalter and others, 162–186. Louisville, Ky.: Westminster/John Knox Press, 1990.

Stigall, Robert. "The Presbyterian Hymnal: Musical Concerns." In "The Presbyterian Hymnal," edited by Peter C. Bower. *Reformed Liturgy and Music* 24 (spring 1990): 69–71.

Stout, Barbara M. "What About the New Hymnal?" In "The Presbyterian Hymnal," edited by Peter C. Bower. *Reformed Liturgy and Music* 24 (spring 1990): 84–85.

Sydnor, James Rawlings. "Sing a New Song to the Lord: An Historical Survey of American Presbyterian Hymnals." *American Presbyterians* 68, no. 1 (1990): 1–13.

———. "Why a New Hymnal?" In "The Presbyterian Hymnal," edited by Peter C. Bower. *Reformed Liturgy and Music* 24 (spring 1990): 58–59.

Weaver, John. "Introducing Service Music." In "The Presbyterian Hymnal," edited by Peter C. Bower. *Reformed Liturgy and Music* 24 (spring 1990): 75–76.

Youngs, Sharon K. "Textual Concerns." In "The Presbyterian Hymnal," edited by Peter C. Bower. *Reformed Liturgy and Music* 24 (spring 1990): 66–68.

Quaker (*see* Friends)

Reformed

Anderson, Fred R. "Three New Voices: Singing God's Song [Christian Reformed Psalter Hymnal; United Methodist Hymnal; Presbyterian Hymnal]." *Theology Today* 47 (October 1990): 260–272.

Brumm, James L. H. "Coming to America: RCA Hymnals in the Eighteenth and Nineteenth Centuries." *The Hymn* 41, no. 1 (January 1990): 27–33.

———. "John Henry Livingston, Unlikely Hymnal Pioneer." *The Hymn* 48, no. 4 (October 1997): 36–43.

Leaver, Robin. "Three Hymnals: Different Denominational Emphasis but One Song?" *Worship* 61 (January 1987): 45–60.

Westermeyer, Paul. "German Reformed Hymnody in the United States." *The Hymn* 31, no. 2 (April 1980): 89–94+; no. 3 (July 1980): 200–204+.

———. "Lineaments of the Reformed and Lutheran Traditions: Liturgy and Hymnody in Nineteenth-Century Pennsylvania." *Church Music* 80 (1980): 2–22.

Zuiderveld, Rudolf. "Ethnic Hymnody Series: Some Musical Traditions in Dutch Reformed Churches in America." *The Hymn* 36, no. 3 (July 1985): 23–25.

Reorganized Church of Jesus Christ of Latter-day Saints (*see* Community of Christ)

Schwenkfelder

Seipt, Allen Anders. *Schwenkfelder Hymnology and the Sources of the First Schwenkfelder Hymn-Book Printed in America*. Philadelphia: Americana Germanica Press, 1909.

Seventh-day Adventist

Hooper, Wayne. "The Making of the Seventh-Day Adventist Hymnal." *Adventist Heritage* 14, no. 1 (1991): 12–17.

Peterson, Orval A. "An Analysis of Twenty Hymns of the Seventh-Day Adventist Church Hymnal." Master's thesis, San Jose State College, 1959.

Pierce, Charles. "A History of Music and of Music Education of the Seventh-Day Adventist Church." D.M.A. diss., Catholic University of America, 1976.

Wildman, Linda. *A Bibliography of Sources on Seventh-Day Adventist Hymnody*. N.p.: n.p., 1990.

———. *Seventh-Day Adventist Hymnists as Represented in Four Major Hymnals:* The Seventh-Day Adventist Hymn and Tune Book for Use in Divine Worship, 1886; Christ in Song for All Religious Services, 1908; The Church Hymnal: Official Hymnal of the Seventh-Day Adventist Church, 1941; The Seventh-Day Adventist Hymnal, 1985. N.p.: n.p., 1990.

Unitarian Universalist

Box, Howard. "Hymnals and Humanists?" *Religious Humanism* 23, no. 1 (winter 1989): 32–36.

Mirchanani, Sharon. "Looking for Diversity and Inclusiveness in the Music of the Unitarian Universalist Church." *The Hymn* 51, no. 2 (2000): 24–27.

Wagner, Chris. *Thirteen Ways of Looking at a UU Hymnal: A Guide for Lay and Professional UU Worship Leaders for Expanding Your Use of Singing the Living Tradition.* Rev. 1st ed. Columbus, Ohio: Chris Wagner, 1998.

United Church of Canada

Barthel, Alan. "*Voices United:* The Hymn and Worship Book of the United Church of Canada." *The Hymn* 50, no. 2 (April 1999): 8–11.

Harding, Bruce. "Singing Our Faith: The Music of *Voices United.*" *Touchstone* 15 (January 1997): 26–37.

Hobbs, R. Gerald. "The Gifts of Every Time and Place." *Touchstone* 8 (September 1990): 2–4.

Riel, Jennifer. "Voices in Harmony: Methodist and Presbyterian Hymn Books prior to Church Union." *Touchstone* 15 (January 1997): 38–44.

Semple, Stuart. "The Hymn Book Revisited." *Touchstone* 4 (January 1986): 40–45.

Wilson, John. "Hymns for Today and Tomorrow." *English Church Music* (1972): 36–50.

United Church of Christ

Beier, Theodor Emil. "The Analysis, Synopsis, and Development of the English Hymnals of the Evangelical Synod of North America." B.Div. thesis, Eden Theological Seminary, 1932.

Christensen, Richard L., ed. *How Shall We Sing the Lord's Song? An Assessment of* The New Century Hymnal. Centerville, Mass.: Confessing Christ, 1997.

Hinke, William John. *The Early German Hymn Books of the Reformed Church in the United States*. [Philadelphia]: Presbyterian Historical Society, 1907.

Meier, Judith A. H. *The Significance of Mercersburg Theology on the* New Century Hymnal. N.p.: n.p., 1999.

Rehwalt, Peter W. "Splashing in the Ever-Rolling Stream: The Arts at Work in *The United Methodist Hymnal* and *The New Century Hymnal*." *The Hymn* 52, no. 4 (October, 2001): 19–29.

Riggs, John W. "Traditions, Tradition, and Liturgical Norms: the United Church of Christ Book of Worship." *Worship* 62 (January 1988): 58–72.

Young, Carl R. "*The New Century Hymnal,* 1995." *The Hymn* 48, no. 2 (April 1997): 25–38.

STUDIES OF HYMNALS ACROSS DENOMINATIONS

Beckwith, John. "Tunebooks and Hymnals in Canada, 1801–1939." *American Music* (summer 1988): 193.

Blycker, Philip Walter. "A Critical Analysis of Selected Spanish-Language Hymnals Used by Evangelical Churches in Mesoamerica, 1952–1992." D.M.A. diss., Southwestern Baptist Theological Seminary, 1997.

Buono, John Wesley. "Common Elements in the Hymnals of the Major Protestant Denominations in America." Ph.D. diss., University of Pittsburgh, 1952.

Clark, Keith C. "A Bibliography of Hymnbooks and Companions to Hymnals: American, Canadian, and English." *The Hymn* 30, no. 3 (July 1979): 205–209; 30, no. 4 (October 1979): 269–272+; 31, no. 1 (January 1980): 41–47+.

Coker, Joe L. "A Bibliography of American Temperance Hymnals, 1835–1934." *The Hymn* 51, no. 2 (April 2000): 28–36.

Costen, Melva Wilson. "Published Hymnals in the Afro-American Tradition." *The Hymn* 40, no. 1 (January 1989): 7–13.

Edmunds, John. "Hymnal, Church, and Urban Muse." *The Hymn* 17, no. 2 (April 1966): 52–57.

Edwards, Deane. "A Glimpse at Hymnody Today." *The Hymn* 17, no. 1 (January 1966): 12–15.

Eskew, Harry L. "Bibliography of Hymnals in Use in American and Canadian Churches." *The Hymn* 37, no. 2 (1986): 25–30.

Foote, Henry Wilder. *Recent American Hymnody.* The Papers of the Hymn Society, edited by Lindsay B. Longacre, 17. New York: The Hymn Society of America, 1952.

Grindal, Gracia. "Where We Are Now." *The Hymn* 38, no. 4 (October 1987): 22–25.

Hall, Paul M. "The Shape-Note Hymnals and Tune Books of Ruebush-Kieffer Company Music Publishers in Virginia." *The Hymn* 22, no. 3 (July 1971): 69–76.

Havens, Thomas W. "Welsh Hymn Tunes in Selected United States Hymnals of the Twentieth Century: A Historical and Analytical Study." Master's thesis, Southwestern Baptist Theological Seminary, 1985.

Hawn, C. Michael. "The Consultation on Ecumenical Hymnody: An Evaluation of Its Influence in Selected English Language Hymnals Published in the United States and Canada since 1976." *The Hymn* 47, no. 2 (1996): 26–30+.

———. "A Survey of Trends in Recent Protestant Hymnals: African-American Spirituals, Hymns, and Gospel Songs." *The Hymn* 43, no. 1 (1992): 21–28.

———. "A Survey of Trends in Recent Protestant Hymnals: International Hymnody." *The Hymn* 42, no. 4 (1991): 24–32.

———. "A Survey of Trends in Recent Protestant Hymnals: Mainstream America, British, and Canadian Hymnody since 1960." *The Hymn* 42, no. 3 (1991): 17–25.

———. "Vox Populi: Developing Global Song in the Northern World." The Hymn 46, no. 4 (1995): 28–37.

Higginson, J. Vincent. *Hymnody in the American Indian Missions.* The Papers of the Hymn Society, edited by William Watkins Reid, 18. New York: The Hymn Society of America, 1954.

Jackson-Brown, Irene V. "The Rise of Black Hymnals." In *African-American Religion: Research Problems and Resources for the 1990s,* 98–106. New York: Schomberg Center for Research in Black Culture, 1990.

———. "Afro-American Sacred Song in the Nineteenth Century." *The Black Perspective in Music* 4, no. 1 (spring 1976): 22–38.

Johnson, Bryan. "A Study of Youth Hymnals since 1900." Master's thesis, General Assembly's Training School for Lay Workers, 1939.

Leaver, Robin A. "Hymnals, Hymnal Companions, and Collection Development." *Notes* 47, no. 2 (December 1990): 331–354.

Lindsley, Charles Edward. "Early Nineteenth-Century American Collections of Sacred Choral Music, 1800–1810. I: An Historical Survey of Tune-Book Production to 1810; II: An Annotated Bibliography of Tune-Books, 1800–1810." Ph.D. diss., University of Iowa, 1968.

McCoy, Steven Lee. "Topical Hymnal: A Thematic Extraction." D.M.A. diss., University of Missouri, 1993.

McKellar, Hugh D. "Toronto and Hymnody." *The Hymn* 37, no. 3 (July 1986): 8–13.

Miller, Ronald L. "Contemporary Authors and Hymns as Represented in Ten Recent Hymnals." *The Hymn* 48, no. 2 (April 1997): 39–42.

Music, David W. "Wesley Hymns in Early American Hymnals and Tunebooks." *The Hymn* 39, no. 4 (1988): 37–42.

Nichols, Kathryn L. "A Bibliography of Braille Hymnals." *The Hymn* 42, no. 2 (1991): 27–30.

———. "A Bibliography of Large Print Hymnals." *The Hymn* 42, no. 3 (1991): 29–30.

Olivieri, Luis A. "The Music of the Protestant Hymnals Used in Puerto Rico." Master's thesis, Boston University, 1976.

Rogal, Samuel J. *The Children's Jubilee: A Bibliographical Survey of Hymnals for Infants, Youth, and Sunday Schools Published in Britain and America, 1655—1900*. Westport, Conn.: Greenwood Press, 1983.

———. "Major Hymnals Published in America: 1640–1900." *Princeton Seminary Bulletin* 61 (summer 1968): 77–92.

Rushing, James Kenneth. "The Acceptance of Negro Spirituals into Major Twentieth-Century American Hymnals." Master's thesis, Southwestern Baptist Theological Seminary, 1986.

Sharp, Timothy. "The Decade of the Hymnal, 1982–1992: Choral Piety and Belief, Hardbound." *The Choral Journal* 32, no. 9 (April 1992): 31–44.

Sharrock, Barry. "A Survey of the Texts and Music of Representative New Hymns As Found in Selected American Protestant Hymnals." Master's thesis, Southern Baptist Theological Seminary, 1975.

A Short Bibliography for the Study of Hymns. The Papers of the Hymn Society, edited by James Sydnor Rawlings, 25. New York: The Hymn Society of America, 1964.

Sidebothom, Timothy James. "Music in the Marriage Rites of Mainline Protestantism (1978–1983): A Theological, Liturgical, and Cultural Analysis." Ph.D. diss., Drew University, 1997.

Simpson, William D. "The Hymns of the Hymn Society of America since 1949 and Their Inclusion in Major American and Canadian Hymnals." Master's thesis, Southwestern Baptist Theological Seminary, 1983.

Southern, Eileen. "Hymnals of the Black Church." *Journal of the Interdenominational Theological Center* 14 (fall–spring 1986–1987): 127–140.

Spencer, Jon Michael. *Black Hymnody: A Hymnological History of the African-American Church.* Knoxville: University of Tennessee Press, 1992.

Stillman, A. K. "Beyond Bibliography: Interpreting Hawaiian-Language Protestant Hymn Imprints." *Ethnomusicology* 40, no. 3 (1996): 469–488.

Sydnor, James Rawlings. "Twentieth-Century Hymnody in the United States." *Papers of the Hymn Society* 24 (1962): 28–41.

Thomas, Georgia Fletcher. "The History of the Shape-Note Hymnal from 1800 to the Present." Master's thesis, Kent State University, 1969.

Thompson, Colin P., and Gordon S. Wakefield. "The Arranging of Hymn Books." In *Singing the Faith,* edited by Charles Robertson, 89–111. Norwich, England: The Canterbury Press, 1990.

Voogt, Mary Jane. "Editorial Perspectives in Sunday School Hymnals Published between 1859 and 1898 which Reflect Educational Philosophy and Practice." *Missouri Journal of Research in Music Education* 4, no. 5 (1981): 52–72.

———. "A Survey of Selected Protestant American Sunday School Hymnals Published from 1826 to 1977." Master's thesis, Conservatory of Music, University of Missouri-Kansas City, 1981.

Washburn, Al. "Bibliography of Hymnals in Print for Children and Youth." *The Hymn* 30, no. 1 (January 1979): 36–38+.

Westermeyer, Paul. "Twentieth-Century American Hymnody and Church Music." In *New Dimensions in American Religious History: Essays in Honor of Martin E. Marty,* edited by Jay P. Dolan and James P. Wind, 175–207. Grand Rapids, Mich.: William B. Eerdmans, 1993.

Young, Carlton R. "Ethnic Minority Hymns in United States Mainline Protestant Hymnals 1940–1995: Some Qualitative Considerations." *The Hymn* 49, no. 3 (July 1998): 17–27.

DESCRIPTIONS OF HYMNAL COLLECTIONS

Anderson, Frank J., ed. *Hymns and Hymnody*. Special Collections Checklists, no. 1. Spartanburg, S.C.: Wofford College Library, 1970.

Backus, Edythe. *Catalogue of Music in the Huntington Library Printed before 1801*. San Marino, Calif.: The Huntington Library, 1949.

———. "The Music Resources of the Huntington Library." *Notes* 14 (1942): 27–35.

Ball, Mark. [*A List of Hymnals in the Spurgeon Collection, William Jewell College*]. Liberty, Mo.: William Jewell College, 1978.

Bowman, Doris Gene. "A List and Description of Hymn Books in the Southern Baptist Theological Seminary Library in 1953." Ph.D. diss., Southern Baptist Theological Seminary, 1953.

Boston Public Library. *Dictionary Catalog of the Music Collection*. Boston: G. K. Hall, 1972–.

———. *Dictionary Catalog of the Music Collection: Supplement*. Boston: G. K. Hall, 1977–.

———. *Landmarks in Music*. Boston: Boston Public Library, 1924.

Cook, Harold E. "Collation of the Manuscript Hymnals." In *Shaker Music: A Manifestation of American Folk Culture*. Lewisburg, Pa.: Bucknell University Press, 1973. *Libraries included:* Collection of Author, Connecticut State Library, Grosvenor Library (now Buffalo and Erie County Public Library), Library of Congress, New York State Library, Shaker Community (Hancock, Mass.), Shaker Community (New Lebanon, N.Y.), University of Michigan, Western Reserve Historical Society (Cleveland), and Williams College (Williamstown, Mass.).

Daniel, Ann Hayes. "The Sellers-Martin Hymnal Collection: A Source for the History of Gospel Hymnody." Master's thesis, New Orleans Baptist Theological Seminary, 1970.

Detrick, Daniel A. "The Hymn Society of America's Collection of Hymnals and Hymnological Materials: An Annotated Index." Master's thesis, Texas Christian University, 1988.

Ellinwood, Leonard, and Anne Woodward Douglas. "The Douglas Collection in the Washington Cathedral Library." *The Papers of the Hymn Society* 23 (1958): 36–72.

Eskew, Harry. *British and American Psalters, Hymnals, and Tune Books on the Tulane University Campus*. [New Orleans]: n.p., 1962.

Fouts, Gordon E. "Music Instruction in America to around 1830: As Suggested by the Hartzler Collection of Early Protestant American Tune Books." Ph.D. diss., University of Iowa, 1968.

Horst, Irvin. "Singers Glen, Virginia, Imprints, 1847–1878: A Checklist." *Eastern Mennonite College Bulletin* 44, no. 2 (1965): 6–14. *Libraries included:* Bridgewater College, Lutheran Theological Southern Seminary, Menno Simons Historical Library and Archives (Eastern Mennonite University), Rockingham Public Library (now Massanutten Regional Library, Harrisonburg, Va.), and Alderman Library (University of Virginia, Charlottesville).

Hymnody Collection. Mankato, Minn.: Bethany Lutheran Theological Seminary, 1978.

Jackson, George Pullen. *Index to the George Pullen Jackson Collection of Southern Hymnody*. Nashville, Tenn.: Joint University Libraries, 1953.

John, Robert W. *A Catalogue of the Irving Lowens Collection of Tune Books*. Winston-Salem, N.C.: Moravian Music Foundation, 1971.

Judd, Bernice, et al. *Hawaiian Language Imprints 1822–1899: A Bibliography*. Honolulu: Hawaiian Mission Children's Society, 1978.

Krohn, Ernst C. "A Check List of Editions of *The Missouri Harmony*." In *Missouri Music,* 200–225. New York: Da Capo Press, 1971. Originally published in *Bulletin of the Missouri Historical Society* 6, no. 3 (April 1950): 372–399.

Krummel, Donald. "The Newberry Library, Chicago." *Fontes Artis Musicae* 16, no. 3 (July–December 1969): 119–124.

Krummel, Donald, ed. *Bibliographical Inventory to the Early Music in the Newberry Library*. Chicago: G. K. Hall, 1977.

Library of Congress, Music Division, Archive of Folk Song. *A Brief List of Materials Relating to Shaker Music*. [Washington, D.C.?]: The Archive, 1967.

Lindsley, Charles Edward. "An Important Tunebook Collection in California." *Notes* 29, no. 4 (June 1973): 671–674. Describes Claremont Colleges' McCutchan Collection.

Lowens, Irving. "The Warrington Collection: A Research Adventure at Case Memorial Library." In *Music and Musicians in Early America,* 272–278. New York: W. W. Norton, 1964.

Luther, M. C. "The P. Boyd Smith Hymnology Collection at California Baptist College." *The Hymn* 46, no. 2 (1995): 52.

Meyer, Henry Edwin, William Carrington Finch, and Norma Siviter Assadourian. *Special Collections in Methodism: William C. Finch,*

John C. Granbery, Henry E. Meyer. Georgetown, Tex.: A. Frank Smith, Jr. Library Center, Southwestern University, 1990.

Minniear, John. "An Annotated Catalogue of the Rare Music in the Baylor University Library." Master's thesis, Baylor University, 1963. Supplements added in 1969, 1972, and 1980.

Monroe, Anita Fletcher. "Tune Books in the Irving Lowens Musical Americana Collection: An Historical and Bibliographic Study." ACRL Microform Series, no. 176. Master's thesis, University of North Carolina at Chapel Hill, 1966.

New York Public Library Research Libraries. Dictionary Catalog of the Music Collection. 2nd ed. Boston, Mass.: G. K. Hall, 1982–.

"NPM [National Association of Pastoral Musicians] Hymnal Library: Current Holdings." *Pastoral Music* 20, no. 5 (1996): 10–11.

O'Meara, Eva J. "The Lowell Mason Library." *Notes* 28, no. 2 (December 1971): 197–208.

———. "The Lowell Mason Library of Music." *The Yale University Library Gazette* 40, no. 2 (October 1965): 57–74.

Pike, Kermit J., comp. *A Guide to Major Manuscript Collections Accessioned and Processed by the Library of the Western Reserve Historical Society since 1970*. Cleveland, Ohio: Western Reserve Historical Society, 1987.

Powell, Paul. "Treasures of the Benson Collection." *The Hymn* 45, no. 1 (1994): 39; no. 2 (1994): 44; no. 3 (1994): 29; no. 4 (1994): 56.

Ralston, Jack L. *With A Voice of Singing: A Selective Bibliography of Master Works from the Clark Hymnology Collection*. 2nd ed. Virginia Beach, Va.: CBN University, 1989.

Raymond, Gillian. *SDA Hymn and Songbook Collection, James White Library, Andrews University: English Bibliography (Chronological)*. N.p: n.p., 1990.

———. *SDA Hymn and Songbook Collection, James White Library, Andrews University: Foreign Bibliography (by Language and Title)*. N.p: n.p., 1990.

Richmond, Mary, comp. *Shaker Literature: A Bibliography*. Vol. 1. Hancock, Mass.: Shaker Community, Inc., 1977. Collections whose holdings are listed in the "Music Leaflets" section (152–155): American Antiquarian Society, Berkshire Athenaeum (Pittsfield, Mass.), Fruitlands Museums (Harvard, Mass.), Grosvenor Reference Division (now Buffalo and Erie County Public Library), New York Public Library, New York State Library, Newberry Library, Shaker Museum (Old Chatham, N.Y.), State Historical Society (Madison, Wis.), Western Kentucky University, Western Reserve Historical Society (Cleveland), and Williams

Historical Society (Cleveland), and Williams College (Williamstown, Mass.).

"The Robert H. Mitchell Hymnological Library." *The Hymn* 47, no. 2 (1996): 47–48.

Sax, Margaret. *Billings to Joplin: Popular Music in Nineteenth-Century America: An Exhibition Arranged and Described by Margaret F. Sax*. Hartford, Conn.: Watkinson Library, 1980.

———. *Music in the Watkinson Library*. 2nd ed., rev. Hartford, Conn.: Watkinson Library, Trinity College, 1986.

Schalk, Carl. *Hymnals and Chorale Books of the Klinck Memorial Library*. River Forest, Ill.: Concordia Teachers College, 1975.

Scherer, Robert W. *Scherer's Bamforth Checklist*. Hollywood, Fla.: n.p., 1973.

See, Ruth D., comp. *Historical Foundation Materials Concerning Early American Church Music from the Colonies to the Mid-Nineteenth Century*. Montreat, N.C.: The Historical Foundation of the Presbyterian and Reformed Churches, 1975.

A Short Bibliography for the Study of Hymns. The Papers of the Hymn Society, edited by James Sydnor Rawlings, 25–30. New York: The Hymn Society of America, 1964. *Libraries included:* The Baker Collection (Duke University, Durham, N.C.), The Benson Collection (Princeton Seminary, N.J.), The Douglas Collection (Washington Cathedral, Washington, D.C.), The Hartford Warrington Collection (Hartford Seminary Foundation, Hartford, Conn.) The Hymn Society of America Collection (Union Theological Seminary, New York, N.Y.), The Library of Congress Collection (Library of Congress, Washington, D.C.), The Peters Memorial Library (Moravian Music Foundation, Winston–Salem, N.C.), The Pittsburgh Warrington Collection (Pittsburgh Theological Seminary, Pittsburgh, Pa.).

Showalter, Grace I. *The Music Books of Ruebush and Kieffer, 1866–1942*. Virginia State Library Publications, no. 41. Richmond: Virginia State Library, 1983. *Libraries included:* Bridgewater College Library (Bridgewater, Va.), Eastern Mennonite College Library (Harrisonburg, Va.), Library of Congress, James Madison College (Harrisonburg, Va.), Joseph H. Meyerhoeffer (Dayton, Va.), Rockingham County Historical Society (Harrisonburg, Va.), Rockingham County Public Library (Harrisonburg, Va.), University of Virginia Library (Charlottesville, Va.), and Virginia State Library (Richmond, Va.).

Sims, Phillip and Scotty Gray. "Psalters of the Maurice Frost Collection at Southwestern Baptist Theological Seminary." *The Hymn* 30, no. 2 (April 1979): 89–92+.

Smoak, A. Merril. "Hymnal Collections in the Greater Los Angeles Area." *The Hymn* 30, no. 2 (1979): 102–105. *Libraries included:* University of California at Los Angeles (George Pullen Jackson Collection of Southern Hymnody), Claremont Colleges (McCutchan Collection of Hymnology), and the Huntington Library (San Marino, Calif.).

Springer, Nelson P., and A. J. Klassen, comps. *Mennonite Bibliography, 1631-1961*. Vol. 2 [North America]. Scottdale, Pa.: Herald Press, 1977. *Libraries included:* Associated Mennonite Biblical Seminaries (now Associated Mennonite Biblical Seminary, Elkhart, Ind.), Canadian Mennonite Bible College (Winnipeg, Manitoba), Hiebert Library (Biblical Seminary-Fresno Pacific College, Fresno, Calif.), Historical Society of Pennsylvania (Philadelphia), Menno Simons Library and Archives (Eastern Mennonite University, Va.), Mennonite Brethren Bible College (Winnipeg, Man.), Mennonite Historical Library (Goshen, Ind.), Mennonite Historical Library (Bluffton, Ohio), Mennonite Library and Archives (Bethel College, Kans.), New York Public Library, Tabor College (Hillsboro, Kans.), and Verenigde Doopsgezinde Gemeente (now in the Universiteits-Bibliotheek, Amsterdam).

Stinnecke Maryland Episcopal Library. *Catalogue of Liturgies, Liturgical Works, Books of Private Devotion, Hymnals and Collections of Hymns . . . The Legacy of W. R. Whittingham, Bishop of Maryland*. Baltimore: n.p., 1881.

Thomason, Jean Healan. *Shaker Manuscript Hymnals from South Union, Kentucky*. Kentucky Folklore Series, no. 3. Bowling Green: Kentucky Folklore Society, 1967. *Libraries included:* Kentucky Library (Western Kentucky University).

Van Burkalow, Anastasia. "The Hymn Society's Collection in the Library of New York's Union Theological Seminary." *The Hymn* 35, no. 3 (July 1984): 164–167.

Voigt, Louis. *Hymnbooks at Wittenberg: A Classified Catalog of the Collections of Hamma School of Theology*. Springfield, Ohio: Chantry Music Press, 1975.

"The Warrington-Pratt-Soule Collection of Hymnody and Psalmody." *The Hymn* 42, no. 1 (1991): 4.

Weadon, D. A. "A Hymnal Tour in Protestant America." *Journal of Church Music* 29 (March 1987): 9–12+.

Weaver, James C. "The Keith C. Clark Hymnal Collection." *The Hymn* 52, no. 3 (2001): 46–47.

Wicklund, Nancy. "The Erik Routley Collection of Books and Hymnals at Talbott Library, Westminster Choir College of Rider University." *The Hymn* 53, no. 4 (October 2002): 46–49.

Zeager, Lloyd. "The Martin E. Ressler Hymnology Collections." *The Hymn* 46, no. 1 (1995): 44.

REFERENCE WORKS IN HYMNOLOGY

Britton, Allen Perdue, Irving Lowens, and Richard Crawford. *American Sacred Music Imprints, 1698-1810*. Worcester, Mass.: American Antiquarian Society, 1990.

Dictionary of American Hymnology Project. In process at Oberlin College. Address queries to Mary L. VanDyke, DAH Project, Oberlin College Library, Oberlin, Ohio 44074, (216) 775-8622, or to dhymns@oberlin.edu. See also: www.oberlin.edu/library/libn collect/DAH.html.

Ellinwood, Leonard W. *Bibliography of American Hymnals, Compiled from the Files of the Dictionary of American Hymnology: A Project of the Hymn Society of America, Inc*. New York: University Music Editions, 1983.

Foote, Henry W. *Three Centuries of American Hymnody*. Hamden, Conn.: Archon Books, 1968.

Julian, John, ed. *A Dictionary of Hymnology*. Rev. ed. London: J. Murray, 1907.

Krummel, D. W., and others. *Resources of American History: A Directory of Source Materials from Colonial Times to World War II*. Urbana: University of Illinois Press, 1981.

Landes, W. Daniel. *The Electronic Encyclopedia of Hymnology*. Ver. 2.0. Nashville, Tenn.: Putnam Graphics & Media Design, 2000.

Leaver, Robin A. *A Hymn Book Survey, 1962—80*. Grove Worship Series, no. 71. Bramcote, Notts.: Grove Books, 1980.

Leaver, Robin A., ed. *Bibliotheca Hymnologica (1890)*. London: Charles Higham, 1981.

Metcalf, Frank J. *American Psalmody, or, Titles of Books Containing Tunes Printed in America from 1721 to 1820*. Heartman's Historical Series, no. 27. New York: C. F. Heartman, 1917.

Music, David W. *Christian Hymnody in Twentieth-Century Britain and America: An Annotated Bibliography*. Bibliographies and Indexes in Religious Studies, no. 52. Westport, Conn.: Greenwood Press, 2001.

———. *Hymnology: A Collection of Source Readings*. Studies in Liturgical Musicology, no. 4. Lanham, Md.: Scarecrow Press, 1996.

Routley, Erik. *An English-Speaking Hymnal Guide*. Collegeville, Minn.: Liturgical Press, 1979.

Stanislaw, Richard J. *A Checklist of Four-Shape Shape-Note Tunebooks*. ISAM Monographs, no. 10. Brooklyn: Institute for Studies in American Music, Dept. of Music, School of Performing Arts, Brooklyn College of the City University of New York, 1978.

Temperley, Nicholas, and Charles G. Manns. *The Hymn Tune Index: A Census of English-Language Hymn Tunes in Printed Sources from 1535 to 1820*. 4 vols. Oxford: Clarendon Press, 1998.

Walker, Edward A., comp. *Hymnals Old and New: An Annotated List of Ninety-Seven Hymnals, Songbooks, and Other Resources*. Washington, D.C.: National Association of Pastoral Musicians, n.d.

Wasson, D. DeWitt, comp. *Hymntune Index and Related Hymn Materials*. 3 vols. Studies in Liturgical Musicology, no. 6. Lanham, Md.: Scarecrow Press, 1998.

Index of Denominations and Religions

Where appropriate, entries for historical denominations reference later denominations into which they merged. By the same token, current and historical denominations are referred to the generic denominational entry when applicable.

For example, the Evangelical United Brethren entry is referred to its denominational successor, the United Methodist Church. Both the Evangelical United Brethren and the United Methodist Church entries are referred to the generic "Methodist" entry.

Because some Evangelical Lutheran Church in America and Lutheran Church–Missouri Synod institutions listed just "Lutheran" as a denomination represented by their collections, all such entries are ultimately grouped under the generic term "Lutheran." All numbers refer to entry numbers.

Index of Hymnal Languages and Places of Origin

The United States and the English language are not included in this index. All numbers refer to entry numbers.

This index is not comprehensive because many very large collections did not mention languages included in their holdings. Other collections simply stated that they had materials in several languages, or listed only a few of the languages represented in their collections. These collections are as follows: 7, 9, 15, 19, 45, 75, 109, 139, 161, 166, 173, 175, 181, 190, 207, 238, 239, 259, 271, 294, 298, 299, 300, and 325.

General Index

All numbers refer to entry numbers.

Index of Chronological Holdings

Please note that chronological holdings were not available for every collection. All numbers refer to entry numbers.

About the Author

Tina Schneider is the reference librarian at The Ohio State University at Lima. A native of Durham, New Hampshire, she earned her B.A. in music at St. Olaf College. She has also received an M.A. in music history from Ohio State and an M.L.S. from Kent State University. She lives in Lima with her husband David and son Quinn.